Nation's Leader for K12 Student Recruitment

THE CUSTOMER IS *NOT ALWAYS* RIGHT!

BUT WE SURE DO NEED THEM.

BEST PRACTICES FOR
Great Customer (Family) Services
Exclusively for Public Schools

BRIAN J. STEPHENS

The Customer is Not Always Right!
© 2022 Brian J. Stephens

ISBN 978-1-66786-456-3

TABLE OF CONTENTS

BIG THANKS

Frankly, I'm absolutely amazed at the people who can sit down in isolation and get their thoughts expressed on paper in a clear, concise manner that people would be interested in reading. They get rid of typos. The grammar and the syntax make sense, which leads to a compelling book that people are excited to read.

I am not one of those people. I'm an old soldier first. Yes, I went to law school, but I readily admit I've never been an outstanding writer. I do like to educate, but without many, many people, I would never be able to produce any kind of document in written form. The due thanks for getting this particular book done are great and wide. Without a full team of people who've helped me create this book; and have helped me develop the experiences necessary to refine the rules over time; and have helped me practice and experiment with ways to increase student populations in public schools, none of this would exist. When you're reading this, if you like the rules, if you think you're learning, realize that there's a big team behind the ideas. That's what gives the information significance, and that is what will continue to refine these concepts over time.

First, the key team members who have helped allow me to build this practice, and have allowed us to invest time, energy, and resources into building a practice to recruit students back to public schools, and that's Paige Walkup and Adrian Bond. Historically, people have had either great or terrible partners. I'm absolutely blessed to have two of the best partners anyone could have in the creation of a new product. Thank you two for allowing me to express my creative vision to find new ways to experiment with helping children find access to what I would consider is the best form of education: traditional public schools.

EmaDella Conners is a newer partner in our office, and her nickname happens to be the Golden Child. That's because it seems like all the products and services she touches get better and better and almost become gold in our eyes. Over the years, her dedication to build this practice has been absolutely second to none. Without her, this service would never have occurred.

I also have to thank the full team at CaissaK12. I started listing them by name but this was starting to turn into an Oscar speech that was going on way too long! Just know that from our Grassroots specialist to our leaders we have and continue to refine our services and these rules.

In addition to our teammates, our clients have taught us unbelievably valuable lessons, and we continue to reform and adjust our rules and the methods with which we recruit and keep students in districts through their great input. As a matter of fact, every single time I go out and teach, I also benefit from learning through districts like longtime partner Fort Bend Independent School District, with Kristoffer Smith and Luis DeArmero guiding efforts to locate and bring students back, and other people like Keith Porter, who also wrote part of the foreword to this book, with Georgia School Superintendents Association. I need to thank Dr. Joris Ray and Dr. Angela Whitelaw at Memphis-Shelby County Schools, who have been great thought leaders in this space with us, having led to consecutive years of four-digit student enrollment increases. We've learned so much from them, and I hope that this continues because together we can all prosper and grow.

I'd be remiss, of course, if I didn't thank my wife, Janelle, for allowing me to spend nights and weekends continuing to craft this book for you. Thanks Honey! Or wait...maybe you just want me out of the house. I'll try and not overthink this.

Thank you to the senior creative editor and writer, adjuster, fixer, complete badass who helped get this book in a readable format, Daphne Maysonet. The fact that she comes in and takes my thoughts—some of them, I'll admit, quite chaotic at times—and helps streamline them into a version for you all to read, is due in no small part to her fantastic ability as a writer. Thank you.

Last, and certainly not least, there is someone that is the key to all this work—Magneto. Magneto (the best dog that you've ever seen) has spent many a weekend sitting at my feet, waiting for me to finish this work, so we could go and play. Thanks, Bud.

FOREWORD

Public education has long served our country by providing free educational opportunities for all students no matter their backgrounds, ethnicities, or social statuses. Although most parents indicate they are pleased with the schools that their children attend as well as the education provided to their children, legislation has been increasingly proposed and subsequently passed into law that encourages parents to consider options separate from public schools. As these funds are diverted from the budgets of school districts throughout the country, educational leaders are challenged to promote the benefits of a vibrant public education system, while appropriately serving all students who enter their facilities. Additionally, the pandemic led to the advent of an emerging market of virtual and homeschool companies and programs to entice parents to consider their products and services.

In *The Customer Is Not Always Right*, Brian Stephens has reminded those who work in the field of education that the services they deliver each day are worthy and essential. In so doing, he articulates strategies of communication and identifies marketing techniques that are both innovative and actionable for educational leaders. Having worked with the author through the years, it is not surprising that the content is direct, concise and substantive.

Mr. Stephens's belief in and advocacy for public schools is evident in the ways in which he has expanded his company CaissaK12 to fill this and other service voids for public education in general and school districts specifically. During the pandemic, he and his company served as an invaluable resource to school superintendents and school boards attempting to navigate contradictory beliefs regarding responses to the crisis. Additionally, he continues to provide quality professional development to school superintendents, district office leaders, and principals on how to effectively communicate with stakeholders, appropriately address crisis (disruption), and positively impact public opinion. *The Customer Is Not Always Right* is an extension of these efforts and an important read for those who lead districts.

Keith Porter, Professional Development Director

Georgia Schools Superintendent Association

HOW TO USE THIS BOOK

In my last book (I have only written one other book, but doesn't it sound better to say last?), I created core rules I ask my team to follow in dealing with the media and disruptions. This book was something I thought of as a best practice manual or quick reference guide. It allowed the reader to choose the section they needed when they needed it. I was grateful for the overwhelming positive feedback on how easy the information was to absorb. After all, the key to great communication is to ensure the message is easy to digest. As such, I have taken the same approach with this guide.

The Customer Is Not Always Right! is a refined methodology based on concepts in *Only Morons Say No Comment.* The focus of this reference manual is to provide accessible solutions to public school district conflicts–those that impact student enrollment, employee satisfaction, the bottom line and the overall district reputation.

My advice for reaping the most benefits from this guide: Start by reading any section introduction you find interesting or relevant to your current conflict. Each introduction and individual rule can be read independently from the others and will provide immediate practical insight on a specific issue. You won't need to read the entire book to gain solutions for your most urgent problem. The byproduct of creating standalone reference rules is duplication of important concepts that apply to different contexts in the world of public school education. As you encounter those core concepts throughout your reading, I hope they stick and become valuable resources for you and your team.

You will gain expertise with every rule you read. In essence, the more of these rules you can commit to memory, the better you will communicate in a manner that recruits and keeps more students, and even builds a positive reputation for your school district.

The real power of this book, however, begins when you see how the rules tie together and work with one another. The better you understand the individual rules, the better you will be at seeing the big picture. With this knowledge, you'll be positioned to build a strategic communications plan that has longer-lasting effects and higher returns than simply implementing individual concepts.

TIP: Keep this book in the bathroom for two reasons: 1. read a single rule at a time–any you want, and 2. since I wrote it, that might be the best room in the house for it.

WHY BELIEVE ANY OF THIS?

There is one part of all my writing that I cannot stand to do, and it's talking about my background. It's talking about my company's background. I don't think that anyone really wants to hear anything about me. I think what they do want is to learn, and they want to grow, and that's the stuff I really get excited about.

But I am wrong. I am completely wrong in this category because every single time I go to present, someone yells at me, "Brian, you have to provide your credentials. So that your students, or the people to whom you're giving a keynote presentation, understand where you're coming from and can frame the conversation." And they're absolutely right, and I'm absolutely wrong. So I am going to frame why we are writing this book on how to recruit students back to public schools versus all the other books you can read out there, marketing material, advertising, whatever it is. What makes us an expert? An expert. I didn't say *the* expert, but we *may* be *the* expert.

Let me frame that out for you in three big buckets.

First and foremost, our company conducts an annual survey of parents and caregivers. We do this to increase our own knowledge base. It's at our cost, and everything about it is designed to learn why parents and caregivers are making a choice to either pick your school or another school. Since it's such a competitive landscape, we really wanted to dig into the research. So first we start with the science. What is the science that lets us know what parents care about? What are the main factors in every region of the country that make them either leave your school or pick your school? This annual report gives us a very deep knowledge into what our targets are, and I know I'm phrasing it in a way that some people would call a little crass, but they are targets. That's our target universe. The people we are trying to communicate with are the decision makers, and those decision makers are parents and caregivers.

Our annual report has taught us a lot. For instance, we know that over the last seven years, parents have started to realize they have choices. They have more options than just charter schools and private schools. Now they have homeschools, virtual schools. The number of parents acknowledging their options has increased from the high 30 percent to the mid-40s. Roughly 43 percent of polled parents nationwide are considering switching schools, and for those in urban areas, that percentage is into the mid-50s. Now, this does not mean that the parents are going to switch schools. It simply means they're considering it. That's good for traditional public schools, and it's bad for traditional public schools. It's really just an opportunity because now you have the opportunity to recruit back.

The second way that we get our information and our knowledge base to help you recruit your students back is we actively secret shop or mystery shop schools around the nation. Now, we don't just shop traditional public schools. We secret shop religious schools, private schools, charter schools, and we even started to secret shop virtual online schools. What is the parent's journey? What is their experience, stem to stern, when they're considering picking a school? We look at lots of different factors that we're going to get into in other sections.

For instance, we look at the first impression the parent gets. How are those impressions communicated? How difficult is the enrollment process? How clean is the website? Is it simple? Is it complex? Are there a lot of broken links? All these things help build the parent's journey, and they either are seeing things they want, or they're seeing things that would make them not want to enroll. We use that information to start breaking down the barriers that would stop potential parents from enrolling in traditional public schools.

The last bucket, and the most important bucket, lets you know exactly who we are as a company and where we're coming from. It's our student recruitment 100% guarantee. I want you to understand that we put our money where our mouth is. Nothing about our student recruitment model is theoretical, hypothetical, or ivory tower in any way, shape, or form. We actively recruit students back, and we do not get paid unless the student physically shows up to school, which then allows the school district to get paid.

I know it seems a little crass, again, to talk about money related to students, but they are your customers, and where the student goes, the money goes. Because we believe in our efforts, and we believe in traditional public school education, and we think it's the best, we only represent public schools. We only get paid when we do our job, and the student shows up. It's a win-win or a win-win-win. The first win is for the students because we believe if we recruit them back, they are going to get a better education. The second win is the school districts because they will have more money coming into their coffers to educate the babies and get people raises. The third win–a smaller win, but it's my win–is CaissaK12's win, where we get paid when you get paid.

This means that for everything we do to recruit students, if it's not done effectively, it's a lose-lose-lose. It's a lose for the student because they're not going to get educated as well. It's going to be a lose to the district because they are not going to get that funding that they so desperately need. My company, CaissaK12 also does not get money, even though we've spent literally tens of thousands of hours recruiting each year for school districts. But we believe in our product. We actively put boots on the ground–door knocks. We make tens of thousands of phone calls. We send tens of hundreds of thousands of emails and text messages and internet ads. We'll even do TV and radio–anything to get the parent excited–and then we follow up and get them enrolled as we work in tandem with the school's communications department. We hand those students off to the school district, and then they complete the enrollment process.

Now, I'll say it again. That's all on our dollar because we believe we will get those students enrolled. So everything that we're going to explain and teach, everything, is us putting–I'm not sure how to say this. It's basically that if I don't do a good job for you, I go broke. I want you to pick up all the tips from all of our education materials, so you can improve and do a better job, so we can improve and do it with you. Every bit of education that we've learned over the near decade we've been representing public schools I'm going to be sharing with you to get you better at recruiting and keeping your students.

That's our background in a nutshell. As far as team members and personalities go here at the office, it is great and wide. We have lawyers. We have mathematicians. We have people with doctorate degrees. We have just great, great, great managers and salespeople, all invested to help public schools. That's where we're coming from. That's our background. Now, I can't wait to teach you how to do it. Thanks for your time.

SECTION I:

PROVIDING GREAT FAMILY (CUSTOMER) SERVICE

Our CaissaK12 team and I get asked to travel around the country to train public school employees on how to provide great customer service. I don't really know what customer service means. I'm a lawyer by trade, and I'm always trying to break down the meaning of words, and maybe I'm being a little pedantic in this regard, but I don't like to think about it as customer service. Just the entire notion means that it's an us versus them. We're here to support them, and they're here to provide us with funds to do our job. That's kind of the traditional customer service model that you see with retail and restaurants and almost every business.

Unfortunately, I think that it does not connect well in the public school space. For roughly 185 years in our modern conceptions of the public school system[1], there was no competition for students. You either went to what the government paid for, traditional public schools, or if you had the means, you could go to a private school. Those were your two primary choices, and that was it. What the schools focused on, and rightly so, I may add, was educating the children and turning them into productive citizens of society.

That was our job for a century—just teaching the children. Then competition came into play. Everything from charter schools and homeschools and, now, virtual schools. In some states, people can choose which public school system to attend, so you may be competing with your neighboring district. This has started to change the dichotomy of how we approach families who go to our schools. They have truly become customers because where the children go, the money follows. I know that it feels crass to talk about the fact that there's a monetary connection to the students. In some districts it's as low as $6,000 per student, and, in others, it's $18,000-$20,000. Either way, it affects your budget, and it affects a public school's ability to educate the children. Simply put, less money means fewer resources. It means fewer computers and support personnel and teachers and staff and desks and, for those of you still buying books, books.

They are customers in a way, but they're also families, and they're our families. We need to start treating them as our families. When you begin to see

---

1 From "A History of Public Schools," by Grace Chen, 2022, *Public School Review*, web.

and treat them as members of your family whom you are charged with teaching and growing, you realize you will recruit and keep more of your students. I'll tell you this: the alternative is dire. The competition is not invested in the past century of education. They have new models based on high marketing, high advertising and really great customer service (whatever that means).

Throughout this learning journey, you will learn how public schools can compete, not only compete but *win* more students than the competition. This is possible because, frankly, I believe you're better than the competition.

Once again, I hate talking about the children in terms of money, but the more we appreciate the fact that money follows them, and the more we start treating them as our teammates, the better we'll be at keeping those students. Every rule that I'm providing to you is about connecting better with people. The customer is not always right. The family members aren't always right. The students aren't always right. (By the way, you're not always right, either. I know that you find that shocking. I hurt somebody's feelings just now. No one's right all the time. I'm not right frequently.) But if we start walking into our relationship with families with a realistic attitude and an understanding that they impact our budget, salaries and public school resources, then we can begin to compromise and connect. If we put parameters around the best practices in dealing with difficult situations, the best practices to tactically recruit students, the best practices to secret shop our schools, the best practices to roleplay handling tough situations to become better, then our customer service will become better.

Through this book, you'll see this common theme: I want you to connect realistically with other human beings in a way that shows you're on their team, and I want you to do this for as long as humanly possible. I believe that through this approach, yes, even if they choose to pick a different school system or learning model, you can get them back. The grass is always greener on the other side of the fence, and new shiny marketing from the competition will attract many of your students. However, based on the national polling information we conduct, we know that there's flux going back and forth between all these schooling options. With incremental growth toward authentically connecting with families, your public school district can be on the receiving end of this spectrum, I believe, for a long time.

Know that we are in the trenches with you because one of our principal jobs here at CaissaK12 is to recruit students. I mean actually do the tactical work of recruiting students back to public schools. This is not a theoretical construct that we're providing. We put boots on the ground. We make hundreds of thousands of phone calls in a year. We knock on doors. We have all these systems to actually recruit those students, and everything that we're going to be discussing and preaching is a way to connect with those families that are our families. It's a proven methodology. I think that that's really the best approach to go forward. I hope you enjoy it.

SECTION II:

RULES TO GET STARTED

RULE 1
SCIENCE BEFORE ART

All too often, I find people tend toward wanting to do all the fun stuff when it comes to running an active campaign to recruit students. They love to discuss what the mailers will look like, what's going to be in the TV commercial and what the visual images will be. It's as if everyone thinks the creative should drive the message, and it's the exact opposite of that. The first thing you need to establish to run any great student recruitment campaign is the science. For instance, at CaissaK12, we conduct an annual nationwide parent and caregiver recruitment and retention poll, so we can learn from them what they want in a school. What is it that drives them to make a choice to either stay or leave?

> **TIP: Read the title of this rule again and again. It doesn't read art before science. Your team will want to reverse this. Don't!**

I would encourage you to begin with asking really important questions that you can actually utilize to begin your recruitment efforts. Let's review an example. One of the first questions that we ask, and I would encourage you to ask, is how likely are you to consider switching your student's school next year? It's simple. It's concise, and it lets you know exactly where you are right now. We know that approximately 43 percent of parents are considering leaving schools nationwide. It doesn't mean that they're going to leave, but we know they're susceptible to being recruited. Now, this is good and bad for traditional public schools. It's bad, because that means a lot of your families are considering leaving, but it's good, because a lot of students that are going to other types of schools are also considering leaving. There's a lot of opportunity in this mix.

One of the second major questions that we like to ask is what are the top concerns you have when picking a school? That question alone gives you almost all the information you need to begin recruitment efforts. We've learned that there are three fundamentals that parents say–year in, year out–across the nation. It doesn't matter what their demographics are. It doesn't matter what their economic status is. Parents all care about the same things. And this is a nationwide survey, of course. I'm encouraging you to do your own science in your own community. We've learned that the caregivers care about safety first. When we first started doing this poll years ago, safety was bullying. Then it became gun violence. Then it became Covid. It's right now beginning to transition back into gun violence. But safety is always among the main drivers that parents care about. They will never pick your school if they don't feel like their children are going to be protected and safe.

The second main driver that we've determined through utilizing science before art is parents want to know that their children are going to be successful. What success means is different to every single parent in the world, but fundamentally they'll fill the word success in with what they think about it. For instance, for me, success was the military, which led me to go get additional degrees after that. For some people, it's a trade school, or it's college, or it's a great job. In short, it really means that the student graduates and doesn't live in their basement forever. Parents want to make sure their children go off and become great people in the universe.

The third point that we've learned through doing this poll is there's a unique parent and caregiver concern in every community. I can't say what it is in your community right now, but you have to do the primary research and actually speak to parents and caregivers to find out. Once you determine what they're interested in and what they want, those points should drive the art. All too often, we start developing messages that have nothing to do with who we're attempting to convert or to whom we're even speaking. If you don't care about what they care about, and you're writing your message points in a vacuum, you'll never connect with them. It's vital that you learn what it is they really want, what they really need, and then you draft your message points based on them and not on what you want.

> **TIP: Focus on the caregivers and what they want, not what you think they want.**

RULE 2

SECRET SHOPPING: BASELINE SERVICE

Several years ago, we were recruiting for multiple districts, and we couldn't quite get why parents weren't coming to tours that we had scheduled. The academics were outstanding at this school. The faculty was fantastic. We had been on the tours. For some reason, approximately 35 percent of participants didn't make the tour time, which was much higher than other schools in that region.

We decided that we would begin secret shopping the school to find out what the barrier was. Once you really start to think about the parent's journey, from stem to stern, all the way back from them sitting at their home discussing what school they may send their child to, all the way down to completing enrollment and the student showing up, you will begin to determine the barriers to a successful enrollment process. Once you then know what those barriers are, you can begin to start getting rid of them, or at least minimizing their impact.

For this scenario, I decided I would personally go and secret shop the school, so I signed up for the tour. I called and scheduled, and everyone was very polite. Their communication was excellent. I set a reasonable time for the tour. I took my daughter who, at the time, happened to be an appropriate age for that school, and I thought that would be a fun experience. As I drove to the school, there were really long lines of all the families dropping their cars off. I go, *that's typical.* Maybe we needed to adjust the start time of the tour, so it's not right when people are dropping their children off. I thought maybe that's a bit of a barrier, but not the biggest barrier that would stop the children from actually enrolling.

I continued to wait in line, and I heard what could only be described as an irking sound in my soul. The crossing guards had whistles, and they were using flags and whistles and directing traffic. I came up, and before I could roll the window down and ask where I needed to go, because I really wasn't sure, the crossing guard began to whistle and blow at me and directed me to go forward, so I went forward. I continued to go forward, and I drove right out past the school, so I had to turn around. Then I'm coming back, and I'm like, that was odd. They directed me away from campus.

Then I came forward, and then another guard whistled and blew and blew and pointed me into another section. Then I went through that little tunnel, and that's the drop off line. I attempted to roll down my window again and say I'm not dropping a student off, but before I could get the words out of my mouth, they began to whistle blow, and then proceeded to yell, "Go! Move forward!" Very hostile. Very aggressive.

Now, had I been anyone else, or had I been an actual parent, it was probably at that point that I would have just left and said, this is not the school for me. I then stopped. I put the car into park. I blocked traffic, and I asked the guard to come over. I said, "Please stop yelling at me. We are a new prospective family. I don't know where to go. Will you help me?" Then he was as charming and as fun and as awesome as any person you'll ever meet in your entire life.

So we changed one thing for that entire school based on that mystery tour, based on that secret shopper. We took the whistles away. Once we took the whistles away, the number of people that showed up to tours got much more in alignment with normal precedent in that community. You'll never know what you'll find when you secret shop your school. When you act like a parent and walk through the journey, you will begin to notice things that you can correct.

TIP: Another way to think about establishing a baseline is reviewing the concept of management by walking around. In 1982, Tom Peters and Robert H. Waterman coined this phrase in their book In Search of Excellence: Lessons from America's Best Run Companies. Peters and Waterman examined hundreds of companies and realized one common thread. Successful companies had leaders who spent much of their time in the field instead of sitting behind their desk. In short, get out, look around and be open to finding problems to resolve.

RULE 3

SECRET SHOPPING: FIRST IMPRESSIONS

When you begin to secret shop your school, the first thing I want you to start to look at with a new eye is the first impression the parent gets. What do they see? Do they see a clean, well-maintained property? Is it fun and lively? Are there pictures of artwork from children, or are there mousetraps sitting at the front door? Is the smoking section for the teachers at the front of the building or where the new parents park? Are there piles of garbage behind the gym?

Also, what happens when they approach the door? Are they let in easily? Does somebody ask them for their ID? Are they exercising proper safety protocols, or is it a relaxed atmosphere that lets people know that you don't really care about the safety and security of their babies?

For instance, one time we were secret shopping a school, and only about 30 percent of the public schools that we went into asked us for our IDs. We reported this to the superintendent, and I basically got chastised and was told, "No, we always ask for the ID." I explained that 70 percent of his schools didn't ask for ID. He told me I was wrong. I then said, "OK, what do you want to do about the schools not asking for ID?" You have to know the truth. I'm not talking about reviewing policies that say you're going to ask for ID. I'm not talking about policies that say put smoking sections behind buildings, or don't have smoking sections at all. You have to analyze and determine what's actually going on.

First impressions truly do matter. Again, I was having another conversation with a different school district, and I said, "We really need to move the smoking sections of all these schools to the back of the facility, because they're smoking right where new parents park." I was told again that we don't have smoking sections in any of our schools. The reality of it was that they did have smoking sections. They were just procedurally not allowed. They were against the rules, but people will do what people do. Your job as the person performing the secret shopping is just to be real with what really happens on your campuses.

TIP: Think about driving into a school. Is the marquee sign out of date? If it's out of date, and it says, "We can't wait for Christmas holidays," or the holiday break, and it's February, and the break's been over for a month and a half, and the sign hasn't been updated, it gives people a bad impression. First impressions matter. Take them seriously.

RULE 4

SECRET SHOPPING: COMMUNICATIONS

All too often, we treat our parents and students with that old adage, "Boy, work would be great if it wasn't for the customers." I've heard too many people at schools make the joke, "Boy, teaching and education sure would be great if we didn't have to deal with the students or the parents." The reality is we do. Where they go, the funds go. It's time we start treating them more like customers, more like our clients, and become their advocates and communicate with them in a fashion that makes them want to communicate back.

I have an entire section of this book dedicated to dealing with difficult people and difficult situations, but when you are secret shopping a school, notice how polite people are. Determine if they're friendly. Do they smile when they're greeted? Do they welcome guests? Or when you get to the front desk, do they continue to talk about their day and ignore you?

I remember one school where we were secret shopping. The prospective family comes in. It was an outstanding first impression. It was an older school, but it was still well maintained, and they had beautiful artwork up. The tour got scheduled in a timely fashion. The person showed up, and instead of being greeted, two teachers were having a discussion about a terrible student in their class. The student may have been a terrible student. They may have been a great student. We don't really know, but what a terrible way to communicate with a potential family–to air all your dirty laundry right out there in front of them in the reception area of your school. If people need to vent–and I think that that's important–they need to go into the back rooms and vent. They need to go and do it in a quiet space, not in front of prospective families.

Another thing that often occurs with communication is human beings, for some reason, love to highlight the things that are going wrong, not the things that are going great. You'll get a tour, or they'll be talking to you about the school, and they'll point out the dirty carpet and the cobwebs and the lack of new band equipment, but they don't highlight the positives. They don't talk about the great academics, their fantastic Teacher of the Year, all the students who are graduating, and how infectious the morale is. People have a tendency to highlight the bad instead of the good. So in order to establish great communications, you really need to process what they are sharing with the parents and caregivers. Are they only highlighting the negative, or are they highlighting the positive?

RULE 5
DESTROY ENROLLMENT BARRIERS

All too often, when we start to evaluate the ability of a school district to recruit new students, we find bureaucratic barriers. These barriers made a lot of sense when they were first established before intense competition for students. This is what happens with laws. Laws just continue to grow and grow, and if you ever want to have a funny afternoon, look at laws from the 1700s, 1800s, even the mid-20th century, and you'll find a lot of laws that are completely out of date but still on the books. They're still laws, but they're not enforced anymore, and they're just kind of out there in the hinter grounds, because no one's ever written a law to nullify them. That's the way it has to happen. Someone has to make the decision to do away with those laws.

Let me give you a few examples of barriers that we've seen in the enrollment process for traditional public schools that stop families from enrolling. Number One: way, way, way too much paperwork on the front end. Now, I understand that you have to get the necessary paperwork in order to get funding from the state and to make sure that all the t's are crossed and i's are dotted. The issue is when you put all that paperwork at the front end. You're not doing what's called micro commitments.

A type of business with great micro commitment examples is the car dealership. Shop for a car, and you'll see how many times a great salesperson attempts to get you to say yes. First they'll start by asking you some general questions: Do you want an SUV or sedan? You'll say a sedan, and then they'll say, "Like this?" They're waiting for you to say yes. If that's a no, that's not quite what I want, they'll ask, "What about this?" Yes. Boom. Your first micro commitment was you've committed to yes, this is the type of car you want.

What they didn't do is ask you to fill out all the paperwork to buy a car on the front end. They don't send you to the finance office to buy a car. What they do is they get you in a car that you said yes to, and then they ask you questions I find ridiculous and that I have a great time saying no to, which are, "Do you like the way the air conditioning feels?" Yeah. They all feel the same. It's all air conditioning. It's a new car. Say no, and watch them just go, *oh, no*. They have no idea where to go. They're trying to get you to say as many yeses as possible, building to the big yes.

Another question they might ask is, "Doesn't the radio sound great? Turn the volume up." It's a radio, and you're driving five miles an hour. Go 70 miles an hour in the car, it might not sound as good, but they don't ask you then. They ask you when you're going slow. "Doesn't it smell good? Do you like the feel of the leather?" They're going to get you yes, yes, yes, then "Would you like to buy? Are you going to buy today?" Then you go, yes.

Another great example of micro commitments, where they're not putting all the paperwork up front, is learning how to fly an airplane. Years ago, my wife said she wanted to learn how to fly, and I said, OK, I'm going to get her a lesson. I drove her out to this small airport, and my daughter and I are there, and we're not getting in that plane with her because she doesn't know how to fly yet. I don't know what they do on the first day. It was amazing to me to see how quick they went from us walking in the door to putting her in a plane and getting her in the sky. It was a matter of minutes, not hours. There was no prep course. There was no reading assignment. There was no video assignment. It was, we're going to get you into a plane *as quickly as possible*. It's exciting. It's fun, and it's more likely to keep you wanting to come back.

I talked to a couple pilots. The program administrators used to do it differently. They used to make you do all this testing, all this written work, all this studying, and then they'd put you in a plane. What they realized is paperwork is not fun, and that's a barrier to people paying you for a pilot license. So they flipped where in the process that barrier appears. They put the barrier further at the end, which meant people were much more vested in the process of learning how to fly.

This got people to show up for far more lessons. Then, once students were committed, then they'd have to complete the paperwork. They put all the tough stuff at the end, after people were committed to getting their licenses.

At public schools, we don't do it that way often. Oftentimes, we require 75 forms of ID, blood tests, and a genetic code. I'm exaggerating, of course, but that is kind of the way that we operate with all these things–because we *used to* be able to do it that way when there was no competition. We could require people to provide all that paperwork on the front end with no repercussions. It wasn't about customer service. It was about getting our files completed the correct way in a timely fashion. I get why somebody required that. You've got to go to school here. You live in the area. We need all this paperwork before the first day of school.

Now the districts that are on the cutting edge of recruiting students, and we work with so many of them, have flipped that script. They get some initial paperwork, a one pager, really brief information. We call it micro commitments. Then that leads down the road to more requests. Finally, in the first week of school or the day before the first day, they can bring the paperwork. In some easy fashion, they can get the paperwork in. Certainly, if you have the ability to get this paperwork online, that's great, but even your websites that won't allow you to fill out an enrollment form until you've checked every box and every link are barriers to getting students in the door. You've got to get them to the party first, and then you can make your big ask. That's one of the barriers we've seen.

The second big enrollment barrier I see is bureaucratic nonsense. We were working with a district, and we had gotten new families to commit to returning to that district, and we persuaded families at charter schools or homeschools to come back to the district. We were pretty excited. However, some of those families were rejected by the district. We sat down with the district and said, let's walk through the process of why these 130 people were rejected. The district was willing to lose 130 students times $10,000 a year for each. I'll let you do the math. That's a lot of money for the district. That's a lot of jobs. That's a lot of resources. I was like, why are they getting rejected exactly?

The first thing we found is a number of them had not returned a library book when they did attend the school. Three, four, five years earlier, they had an outstanding library book. I sat there, and I said, "So we're being really penny wise and pound foolish on all this." Basically, they're worried about the nickels and dimes, and they're not worried about the $10,000. I said, "How much is that library book worth? What's the actual value to the district?" $7.95 or something. I said, "I'll give you $10. I'll just give you $10. Let them enroll and get the $10,000." They were losing $10,000 over a single library book, and I am quite certain someone made this rule for a great reason. I'm sure it was that people were not returning library books, and the schools needed the library books! But this was a time before competition reigned. It was at a time when you could put up barriers because you were going to get families to enroll regardless of the barriers.

The superintendent found this out, and they were like, dump that. We'll eat the book cost, for Pete's sake. Get rid of it. There were a few people in the room who said, "But we've got to get the money for the library book." They just were completely obsessed with the library book fee. I was like, this was put in in a time before competition, and we've got to get rid of that. You can still ask for the book back, but don't stop them from enrolling. Let them enroll first, and then you can hound them to get the old book back or the charge back, but don't do it on the front end where they just go, "Forget this. We committed to coming back. We're going to give you another chance, school district, but you're beating me up over a library book that I don't know where it is. I don't want to deal with you. I'm just going to stay at the homeschool or charter school or wherever." It's a barrier. I still understand why it got created, and I think it was created in the '60s in this case.

Another barrier we found, and this was a different district, not a part of that 130 or so, was the same scenario: A few of the students didn't return a piece of their band uniforms. I, once again, broke down the cost for this piece of uniform. What's the average cost? They go, "That's irrelevant. It's the principle, Brian. It's the principle that people need to learn to return their things." I said, "You're right. I think you're right. People need to learn to live up to what their obligations are. People need to learn to return items that they borrowed, and people need to learn to pay me back when I loan them something." I get it. I'm talking to you, neighbor. I have a neighbor who never returns the stuff I loan him.

I understand that, but you're not going to have any chance to teach them this lesson if they don't go back to your school. Not only are they going to be somewhere else, they've also now taken all their money with them. Remember, that student is worth a certain amount of money to your district, and they have left with it. I guarantee you the amount of money annually that that student is allocated to your school budget is a heck of a lot more than that piece of band uniform.

The third barrier that we've seen frequently that needs to be corrected in traditional public schools is the process of how and when to enroll. I know you don't have unlimited resources. I know that you're at a disadvantage, but we can make some subtle adjustments to make it easier for people to come in and fill out their paperwork. We were working with a district that only does paper form enrollment. You'd love to have paper and online enrollment, but this is what they had the capacity to do, and that's fine. But you could only turn the paperwork in from 9:00-2:30. Most people work and have to be at work at 9:00, and they stay way past 2:30. There were no weekend drop offs. There were no early morning drop offs. There was no evening drop off. So someone had to take time off of work to go and drop a sheet of paper off to someone else. There wasn't even a drop box.

I said, "Doesn't that feel like a barrier that we can fix?" Can't we have a drop box, even if somebody can't be there earlier. Actually, the district came up with a great idea. They went, "Why don't we have somebody stay until 5:00, and we pay them a few bucks an hour to stay till 5:00, 5:30 a couple days a week?" We put that out. Somebody can come in early, and we put a drop box. There were a few easy things they could do to get rid of that barrier of people not having time to drop it off.

I promise you, somebody out there is thinking, what's the big deal to skip off on your lunch break and drop it off? It's probably not a big deal, but if your competition doesn't require it, and they don't have that barrier to the enrollment process, and they will come to you (I'm telling you, some of your competition will get in a car, and they will drive to the prospective new student's homes or work to get the paperwork if that's what they need), then that's what you're up against. That little barrier will really stop you from getting–I can't tell you the percentage of actual number of parents who get flustered and decide not to enroll, but we know that it's more than you think. We know that it's more than one, and isn't it worth $8,000, $9,000, $10,000 to make the system a little bit easier for entry?

Also, talking about enrollment, there was another place with enrollment "hubs," if you will, but they weren't on the weekends, and they weren't in the evenings, and nobody had ever thought about doing that. They just said, our workday is 7:30-3:00, and that's when we want to do it. But that's not what the families need, and you've got to really think about what your targets are interested in and what makes sense for their lives, not what makes sense for your life.

These are some of the biggest enrollment barriers we've seen. I would ask you to evaluate and conduct a parent journey, if you will, and see what it's like to be a parent trying to enroll in your school. Any time you see something that annoys you, see what you could do to adjust it. See what you can do to slightly improve it. I think that even a 5-10 percent adjustment can really go a long way.

TIP: Daphne, my world class editor, thought we needed at least one tip box for each section. Which I disagreed with. Sure, it creates uniformity, but if I didn't have a tip, I didn't want to force it. So this tip box is for you, Daphne.

SECTION III:

RULES FOR DEALING WITH DIFFICULT PEOPLE

Over the last 10 years or so, I've traveled the country and given live seminars on what some people refer to as crisis management. I like to refer to it as disruption management. The truth is it's really just the art of dealing with difficult people. Right now, when I say difficult people, somebody probably popped into your mind, a situation that you just faced. One thing that's true across every school district is that people have unbelievable examples of difficult people yelling and being confrontational. Most of them have not been given the correct tools to deal with these difficult situations and people. Instead, they're taught nonsense. People have been taught complete nonsense about customer service for decades, and it all goes back to this outrageous adage that the customer is always right.

"The customer is always right" is total bunk. You know this, subconsciously and even consciously. There's even a name out there used to mock a person related to this idea. I'm not going to do that because I know some lovely people by that name. We know that customers can be completely wrong and completely irrational, but they can also have real situations that require attention and a resolution. After all, there's an old joke that business would be great if we didn't have to deal with the customers, but we have no choice. We have to keep the good customers, even when they're upset.

Let's take this in the context of parents. Let's be honest. All of us who have been parents have lost our minds a little bit. We have all been difficult people at times. I had a bullying situation with my daughter, who was in middle school. She was not the bully. She's a very quiet little bookish girl. At least, in our opinion. I think that that's the key. In our opinion as parents, she was the victim. Now, in the other parents' view, somebody else was the victim, or there was no victim.

Either way, I was having a conversation with the principal and the counselor, and I got irate. I got upset because I wasn't being heard. I wasn't being listened to, and I did not think the school was going to protect my child. In that situation, I became the difficult person. I think I became the difficult person for a really valid reason, and I'm sure that in many cases, people have had to be difficult just to be heard in real situations.

Now, you have another problem that occurs, which is people being completely irrational. I've heard these stories from school after school, in which parents come in and ask for the moon or the parents are not taking care of their children. The children aren't getting to school, for instance, and won't be promoted to the next grade. The parents are upset and demanding their children be promoted regardless. I mean, those are ridiculous situations that are not the secretary's fault, the clerk's fault, the principal's fault or anyone's fault that's on the front line of K12 education, but they are the ones who get the brunt of the problem. This is totally unfair, and it stinks, but it is going on.

I'm hoping that the next series of rules will help reframe this conversation, and instead of us saying, "the customer is always right, you've got to take it on the chin, you've got to do whatever they want," this gives your team tools allowing them to understand how humans are designed to respond to crisis. We respond to crisis baked into our DNA based on a fight-or-flight impulse every human has. The fight-or-flight mentality, in short, is designed to protect us. In prehistoric times, if we saw something scary, we would either fight it or run from it. Either one was designed to protect us from harm.

Genetically, it's a great thing to have, but in modern society, the fight-or-flight mentality gets us into trouble. The parent is typically not going to jump over the counter. It just almost never happens 99.99 percent of the time. Somebody's upset, and I've been upset, and you've been upset, and we've all been upset, but how do we diffuse that situation and get to a win-win? Once we stop thinking that they're wrong and we're right, or they're crazy and we're great, it's another human being having a difficult time in almost all circumstances. All they're looking for is the opportunity to be heard, connect with a human being, but most of all feel like somebody has their back. They want to feel like someone is going to become their advocate.

Now, becoming an advocate for the parent is different from claiming they're always right. I didn't say that the parent is always right, but are you going to become an advocate and show them why the situation at hand can't be resolved exactly to their wishes or is going to be resolved? Do they feel like they have a teammate instead of an enemy? Families are our clients. In K12, the customer is the parent or caregiver, especially in the lower grades. They make the decisions. We want to keep the good ones, even when they're upset.

How do we become advocates for them and end a situation that was very difficult at the start and resolve it in a more beneficial way? I've attempted to write rules that correspond with the training we give, but I'll let you know this: Reading in a book how to deal with difficult people is not the same as a live-fire exercise, actually practicing how to deal with it. The ways most people practice are not effective. I've attempted to clarify how to roleplay these situations, how to become more of an advocate and less on your heels in these situations, but it takes time, and it does take practice. I hope these rules are the start of your journey and not the end.

RULE 1
IT'S NOT A CRISIS, IT'S A DISRUPTION

Now, this is one of my favorite subjects to do live. You'll notice that I don't call this crisis management. I do a lot of crisis management training. I just don't like the term "crisis management." The term crisis management invokes a level of panic, as if you're not going to get through the crisis. When you hear the word "crisis," it invokes an emotional reaction. It invokes fear, anxiety and stress. It causes you not to get through the situation as smoothly as if you understood that it's a speedbump in life. It is something you're going to get through.

The right mindset helps disruptions, and that's what we're going to get into today. I often think about the very upset parent or caregiver. Sometimes it's the parents making the decision on where their students go; sometimes it's the grandparents or aunts and uncles–caregivers. I'll use parent interchangeably throughout all these series. The world's changed, and many times the caregiver is providing the decisions or gets worked trying to protect their children.

I've been really angry as a dad. I often think of angry parents and what that evokes in the front line warriors at schools. Picture, if you will, either a principal, assistant principal or the front desk people. The front desk people, the clerks and administrative staff, I think, take it on the chin more than anyone else. They are the front door to all these schools. When a person comes in irate, agitated, or stressed out about an issue that's very important to them, that will evoke an emotional reaction. Typically, the emotional reaction it evokes is not good. We like to use the terminology fight, flight or think because that emotional reaction kicks in.

The first rule that we need to set out today is that it's not a crisis. I want everyone who goes through one of my video courses or reads the books and any of our training material, you've gone through every crisis you've ever faced. You've done it. It's funny. A common breakdown of fear is "false emotions appearing real." I like that one. That is what really fear is–when somebody's screaming at you because their child's missing, or you retain their child for another year, so they're not grading up. Maybe it's a really stressful situation like an estranged spouse has come and taken their child out without permission. They have a lot of emotions to work through, and they're real, and they're genuine, and we need to learn to deal with them in a way that doesn't blow the situation up even more.

Really dealing with disruptions quickly and timely will allow you not to have to deal with the problem later on social media or them reporting it to the traditional media or your board, or blowing you up with elected officials and complaints. I want you to learn that you can handle the situation. You can handle this disruption now. Don't put it off because if you do, it's not going to go away. It's typically going to blow up and cost you even more time later.

> **TIP:** The old adage, "If you believe you can, you will; and if you believe you can't, you won't" also works for crisis management. Believe you will get through the issue, and you will!

RULE 2

FIGHT, FLIGHT OR THINK

Now, it's no one's fault that we have the fight-or-flight mentality. For those of you who aren't familiar with this term, let me kind of give you the very brief synopsis on it. It's baked into our core. It's baked into our DNA, our genetic code, that we as human beings want to survive. We want to live. We want to get through the next day. The fight or flight emotional process in our body is designed to keep us safe. It's designed to make sure that we stay alive.

In today's modern society, the fight-flight emotion probably isn't the best reaction to common disruptions and issues. Trust me, 10,000, 15,000, 20,000 years ago, whatever it is, it was a crisis. You hear a scary noise coming from around you, and you think it's something that's going to eat you; you either get a spear to defend yourself and fight it, or you run away. Oftentimes, people respond in this fight-or-flight mentality, and it makes the situation worse in modern society because really we don't need to go and beat up what upsets us. We don't need to run from an angry parent or an angry situation. We need to sit, breathe and think.

I really want you to push fight and flight aside and think. The pro-tip is you need to understand which one you are internally. We all can kind of go a little bit in or out of fight or flight, but you as a human being have one that's a little bit more prevalent in your life. Now, I've asked this throughout the entire nation. I've asked this in other countries, and it's funny. Americans like to believe that we're fighters, generally speaking. They think that being a fighter is a better way to be than a flighter. Generally speaking, people who don't know which one they are will pick fighter when they're actually a flighter. Flighters typically allow stuff to build, and then they do fight. Then they do come overboard. It's like a volcano erupting. When the flighters fight, it is a real fight. Everyone is capable of a fight, if you put them in a corner, but for some reason, we in the United States think that being a fighter is better.

I'm here to let you know, they're both equally bad at dealing with disruption. I am absolutely a fighter in almost all situations, and it is not good. I can accept the fact that I overreact. That's just the truth. When my emotional fight-or-flight response kicks in, I want to beat the tar out of what's causing it, and it's not good. Leaving the situation might actually be better in most situations, just to avoid the conflict. But really what we want you to do here as a modern human is *think*. I want you to start to think.

RULE 3
REALISTIC ATTITUDE

That gets us into this next rule, which is I need you to have–I'm begging you–a realistic attitude. Too often when you're doing customer service training, people will tell you all you need is to smile. Somebody's screaming at you, and some so-called expert tells you to smile and enjoy it and to agree with them? This is the absolute garbage that's proliferated in society today. Not today. It's been 50 years, I think. The customer's always right. A very distinct company set that precedent, and everybody grabbed it. I'm going to tell you right now, the customer is not always right. Sometimes the customer's wrong, wrong, wrong, and you know that instinctively. You know in your heart that everybody can be wrong.

I know I hurt somebody's feelings out there because I said you can be wrong. You can be. We all can be wrong. I'm wrong a ton. It's good to acknowledge that it's realistic to understand that the customer's not always right. When you are training your team, and you're dealing with, let's say, an angry parent, you know the parent isn't always right. I've seen roleplay scenarios at different school districts around the nation. Everyone knows parents can lose their minds, especially if they're trying to bully a situation. This doesn't happen all the time, and most parents' concerns are valid and need to be addressed, but there are lots of occasions when they're not right.

Now, that does not mean you can attack them or run from the situation. It means you still have to deal with that emotional dilemma that's in front of you, that emotional disruption that's in front of you right now. I don't want you to beat it up, and I don't want you to run from it. I want you to sit down and think. They're yelling at me. Let's just use one example. A child not being promoted to the next grade. A lot of districts refer to that as the child has been retained. The parents are really upset, and maybe for a valid reason. Maybe it wasn't made clear why their child's being retained. Maybe the parent was wrong;

they weren't paying attention to all the test scores, and maybe they just don't want their child to be retained because they think it's a poor reflection of them. There could be really good reasons, and there could be really bad reasons why the parent is angry and in your face about it.

First let's talk about the steps to advocate for situations like that, walking in with a realistic attitude. Let's discuss what an unrealistic attitude is because I think that will set the frame. I look at training courses out there, and there are so many telling you to smile and be happy, and to just take it on the chin. I think what that does emotionally after a while is make you feel beaten down. You'll start to say, "How am I supposed to live up to this standard? How am I supposed to survive this if nobody has my back in the face of what can only be characterized in some situations as insanity?" They're nuts. They're crazy. I love to watch videos on YouTube about people in restaurants and airlines, and they've lost their minds. Then we're telling front-line service workers just to take it on the chin.

I found an example of prevailing wisdom outside of the school space: *Six Ways to Handle Difficult People*. The first piece of advice is to respond to whatever they say with another topic. Distract them. Think of how this might work in a public school customer service setting: "Oh, your child has been retained? Yeah, but look at the great new sports complex we just built and the great new weight room. Let's go talk about that." That parent's not going to allow you to change the subject.

Thank them. This is another one of the six points: *thank them* for sharing their concern. That parent doesn't want to be thanked. They want to resolve the issue. My child is being bullied is another one that you'll hear, and rightly so. In some situations the child is actually really being bullied, and I know because I've got a lot of experience dealing with this, just like you do. So according to the second point from these six, you'd say, "Thank you for telling us about the bullying situation." That's not going to get it done.

Another one: confess quickly. "Yeah, you're right. We have no idea why we retained your student. Probably shouldn't have, but it's already done on paper, and you're stuck."

More advice: pity and pray. Feel sorry for them because they are miserable, and pray they learn to stop it. They don't want your pity. You've got to actually deal with the situation. I'm not going to get into a hundred different examples out there where they say smile and take it on the chin, but it's just so annoying. I also think that it's going to cause a lot of your great team members to leave your school. They're going to leave your district.

When we don't support our team members in being realistic in their responses to disruptions, the good ones find other jobs. The good ones start to look for another job, or they can redirect their talents to volunteer work or other activities, but not through trying to build a great school district. You've got to really focus on the realistic attitude. What I want you to do is allow people to be humans and have an emotional response that's appropriate for the situation. We're going to get into that more as we keep clicking through some of these rules.

I do want to give a couple other examples about this realistic attitude, because I think that society in general is plaguing us with unrealistic expectations everywhere we go. It's not just in the customer service space. It's also in society in general. The *origin* of this problem is not social media. I know everyone's going to say, social media caused all these unrealistic expectations. You even go back to the invention of TV and movies and radio. Everyone tries to set higher expectations. I imagine you could go back to the medieval times, and somebody's faking that they have more money than their neighbor does. I guess it's kind of human nature to exaggerate. The advent of social media has made it critical that everyone only puts their best face forward, which is a shame.

You see on Instagram a traveler, and they're put together, and they're organized. They've got their shopping bag, and they've got their little suitcase and their glasses. They just look all pro, and they've got a little latte in their hands, and everything just looks perfect for this Instagram post. In reality, we all know how we travel. It's a mess, right? You're dragging luggage. The kids are screaming. Things are falling out of your bags. You can't find a great coffee place, so instead you eat whatever swill you can find. Hair's a mess. They lose things, and they can't find their wallets. Lines are being held up by other people coughing on them. It's tragic, right?

We see what gets posted on social media, and we think everybody else is doing it right. I'm the only mess. You're not. Everyone can be trainwrecks from time to time. Everyone. I'm going to say it again. Everyone can be trainwrecks from time to time. That's human, right? What's wrong with accepting that as a reality?

There is some hope out there because people in the younger generation, I'm talking about my daughter's–high school and below–understand how much deception there is on social media, and they discount it. They grew up with it, and so they're very suspect, more than the people introduced to it after they were older.

I think about the things that I will say on social media, knowing what I know. As a psychologist and a lawyer, which means I'm questioning everything that I've dealt with, I still get completely susceptible to this stuff. I think about somebody who can do some awesome jump on a bike that I can't do, and what they don't show you is how many times they cut the footage where they wrecked. They don't show you that. They just show the perfect smooth line. They just show you the perfect picture of them on the train traveling, on the airplane. They never post the garbage. That's what's happening. I'm really going to encourage us to continue, with our teammates especially, to push off the unrealistic expectations, what it's like not to be human, and embrace humanity for a change.

RULE 4

AUTHENTIC, NOT PROFESSIONAL

It's OK to be authentic and not professional. In order to become somebody's advocate, you can't be polite. I'm not talking about swearing and screaming, but I do mean showing a little human dignity, a little human emotion. We're taught not to show emotion. We're taught to rely on policies and handbooks and procedures that no one cares about when, for instance, their child wasn't served lunch in the cafeteria for three weeks and didn't eat, or when their child has been held back a grade, or a myriad of other situations. What an upset parent wants to know is that you're upset, too–that it bothers you. When you show genuine human emotion about a situation that's actually sad, they'll believe that you're going to resolve it for them.

Then I think it's OK to show some level of compassion. We're taught by all these experts to be like little robots. "That is very upsetting to me that your child did not get to eat. Let me read my form on what I am supposed to do in the case of a child not eating." I need you to push that stoicism aside, that kind of robotic response, and be real. The child didn't get to eat. Go and show them you care and become their advocate.

People want a connection, they want to know someone else cares. When a customer is upset, they *need* to know you have their back, and sounding professional, stern, or distant simply doesn't connect like a person just being themselves. So you be you!

TIP: If you're authentically a jerk . . . maybe ignore this rule and just be professional.

RULE 5

BECOME
THEIR ADVOCATE

There's an expression in business, "Work would be great if we didn't have to deal with the customers." And while this is funny, it articulates the fundamental belief that it's us vs. them. It's this attitude that makes us react in a manner that does not resolve difficult situations as well as we could if we took the attitude that we are all on the same team—that it's our job to represent them, to be their advocates. Frankly, the sooner we realize we are on the same team as the parents, the sooner we will resolve conflicts in a win-win-win manner: a win for the district, a win for us individually and a win for the families. Truly, only together can we prosper.

How do you become a person's advocate if you can't empathize with them? How do you become a person's advocate if all you want to do is get them out of your area and get on with your life? How do you become their advocate if you think they're full of BS, if you're just agitated? Also, how do you become their advocate if you know that no one on your team is going to support you?

I understand how difficult it is to see people as being on your team when they're "attacking" you. I imagine you working at the front desk of a middle school where you are faced with a small group of angry parents. You are doing great work. It's absolutely required, and you are underpaid (I know you're underpaid). It's terrible. It's hard, but I know you're doing it because you believe in your work, and you're trying to take care of the babies. I've seen this happen in a lot of schools. I've seen this happen in a lot of businesses in general.

The parents are out there fussing at the front desk worker, and maybe the principal sneaks into their office to avoid the conflict. You see other people scamper away without providing support. You're a little thin emotionally because maybe a few people have gotten upset about other things that day.

Where are your teammates? Are they helping you? Is somebody else going to wedge themselves in? In the face of all this, it's extremely difficult to see yourself as an advocate, but please, trust me, once you act like you are on their team, they will believe it and respond in kind.

I think the first thing we have to do is create a culture where we are supporting our teammates by becoming advocates. If you start to set a culture where you're trying to advocate for your own team, taking the next step and advocating for the parents and caregivers becomes easier. Of course the longer you wait to start acting like an advocate for the family, the harder it will be.

TIP: How do you become their advocate if you feel like you're on the opposite side of a barrier? If a person's upset, don't have a physical barrier: a big desk, a wall, a glass. Move toward the person in a shared, comfortable space, yes, on the same side of the barrier. I want you to be safe, but we're not talking about somebody walking in brandishing a weapon. I'm talking about parents upset that their child's being bullied. The parent is upset that their child didn't get lunch that day. They're all very valid emotions, and they're real. If it was you, you'd be upset, too.

Let's take an example and break down how to be an advocate. We received a call weeks ago that a child apparently had not been eating lunch for three weeks, and the parents didn't know that because they didn't receive the email notification that the school was not providing lunch for the next month. Nobody said anything for three weeks. The child didn't say anything. The teachers didn't notice. No email or other reminders went to the parents, saying the school's kitchen was still not working. The fact that the child was not eating was the school's fault. It was also the parent's fault, too, for not reading the email that was sent out. The child suffered regardless of who was to blame.

As you can imagine, when the parent discovered their child hadn't been eating lunch for three weeks, they were upset. I've used this difficult situation as a roleplaying context for practicing becoming an advocate. The first response in the roleplaying that we did was, "Wow, we sent you an email about that." Which emotional response does that sound like? We're going to counterattack like it's your fault. We sent you an email, so you can't be mad at us. That's not how it goes either. "We're super sorry about this." Apology. OK, that didn't fix anything. "We'll make sure it doesn't happen again." It doesn't sound to me like you're not going to make it happen again. It sounds to me like you just don't think it's a big deal. You gave me a flippant apology. You blamed me because I didn't get the email. I didn't read it. Sorry. I get thousands and thousands of emails every day. I can't read them all. Maybe I should have, but I didn't.

Meanwhile, a person suffered. A child suffered because I didn't read my email, and you didn't pay attention to some child in your cafeteria not eating every day. You see how it starts to connect; let's forget about fault. Let's worry about the victim in this case.

If we push fault aside, doesn't this situation upset you? The fact the child didn't eat for three weeks is the issue that needs a remedy, not who was right or wrong. But often we get in a defensive posture. We keep the parents on the other side of a barrier. We're talking to them over a desk, and we say, "We'll fix it. We'll make sure that doesn't happen again. Next time please read your emails." We deflect blame. All these responses are robotic in nature, lack empathy and don't care for the victim or the child. Moreover, none builds long-term trust with the families we serve.

Another rule that you're going to read about further down is always take care of the victim first. What I mean in this case is the child who was not eating is the "harmed individual." Emotionally, it was also the parents and caregivers, but it should also emotionally be you. You should be upset that that child didn't get to eat. Let's call it the harmed individual in this case because we don't want to start labeling people as victims in all cases.

The harmed individual in this case was absolutely the child, so what are we doing to advocate for that child? "I am so sorry that Emily didn't get to eat. That really is upsetting to me. I got to get to the bottom of this, mom, dad. I've got to find out how this happened to make sure it never happens again." Doesn't that just feel like you're their advocate, instead of side-strapping it, silence, or showing you're not paying attention to the situation? You've got to really dig in and become their advocate. But how can you do that if you are stuck on either fight or flight? You want to beat that parent. How dare you start yelling and screaming at me right now? You've evoked an emotional reaction in me. Or you want to run from the situation.

It's important that we get into the right mindset about somebody upset and yelling. Now, I don't expect or want you to be yelled at. I don't think you deserve that in any way, shape or form. But somebody venting—are they venting or are they yelling at you? I know a lot of people right now just said, "They're doing both, Brian." Kind of. I'm really loud all the time. I'm loud, and I am a soldier. People say to me, "You're yelling at me." No, I'm just a loud person. Sometimes you just get loud people. Whatever the case, we have to get recentered. Let them go for a minute. Let them get it out of their system. When we roleplay, we really practice these scenarios a lot. I would encourage you to read the roleplay rules, so you can figure out how to really become their advocates in a stressful situation.

One of the reasons we only represent traditional public schools is—I know this—that you do a better job than anyone else at educating and training our children for the future. I know you do a great job. You don't always market it. You don't always get the training. But I know that you care about the children, and if that's all you're fixated on in all these different scenarios, you're going to make the right answer. What I've learned going to school after school in states from the East Coast to the West Coast is you all know the answers to these issues. We just have to free you up to start advocating for the children. Sometimes advocating for the child is: you're going to be kept at the same grade level another year because you're not ready, but we're going to get you ready. Sometimes advocating for the child is: I cannot believe we didn't feed you. I am now going to be checking every single student every single time that our kitchen's down to make sure that everyone's got food, or we're going to go get you food. That's what real advocacy is all about, and that's where I've got to get you in this scenario.

I want you to have a realistic attitude in all these situations because if you're not letting your people have realistic attitudes, you're setting them up for failure. I think about battles and wars. I was blessed not to have this experience in the military, but I've heard stories in which troopers were set up for failure. They were lied to: You're going to do great. You're going to do great. Knowing that it was bunk. Knowing that people were going to die. We're not going to die in these situations, but I do want you to set realistic expectations because your team will be happier. It'll create a better culture, and you'll create more joy. It'll create a lot more joy in your team members' lives, and I think that's really important.

TIP: Becoming an advocate for a person who emotionally avoids conflict can be really tough, especially if you want to keep their students in your school. People who flee will often just take their children and leave. Therefore, you must deal with the situation at hand even if they do not voice major concerns. To become their advocate, you still want to advocate for resolution of the problem. It's even more important with fleers to slow everything down and really discuss their feelings, which they will only share if they truly believe you care and are empathic to their needs.

I know a lot of you know, but just to be clear, the difference between sympathy and empathy is great. Sympathy means we feel bad for you. Empathy is when we feel the same thing that you feel. Try to put yourself in their shoes, so to speak. That's what empathy is. Empathy is putting yourself in their shoes, like really trying to understand their position. What would I feel like if my child didn't eat for three weeks? How would I react? And remember practice makes perfect . . . or at least better.

TIP: Somebody out there is thinking, Brian, I can't resolve their problems. I don't have the power. Yeah. I know. What you'll find is at almost every level in your life journey you're going to be in a position, even if you are the principal, the chief of staff, the superintendent, an elected board member where you do not have power to resolve the issue at hand. But resolution is *not* always needed, often the person harmed just wants reassurance that somebody's on their side. Being honest and real, and just telling them the truth about a situation is often all that's required. They want to know that somebody's working on it.

Let's take the scenario that someone's child has been kept at the same grade level another year. You don't know the facts. Even if you're the principal, you can't recall from memory the details of every child's academic record. The parent is upset, and they're yelling, "The teacher never responds to me. I never knew about these bad grades. I never knew that this final test was such a big deal, and now you're telling me that because my child got decent grades, and they messed up one test, it's over with. That is bonkers."

In this scenario, you may not have the power to promote their child, but you can start to dig in and become a little investigator, become their lawyer, so to speak. Just knowing you are really looking into the matter because you care is enough–not that you actually promoted their child. Of course, not all people will appreciate that you tried. Of course, some people can never be pleased...there are no rules for these people, just let them go!

UNDERSTAND THE SIX EMOTIONAL RESPONSES TO A CRISIS

In order to become an advocate, we have to continue to break down our common emotional responses to conflict or a crisis. This is beyond fight or flight (*see rule above*) and digs into the ways we all deal with conflict in real time. Experts at dealing with crises agree that there are basically six emotional responses to a disruption, and a seventh non-emotional one. It doesn't really matter the level of disruption. It could be anything from a child being held back to a bullying situation to a tragedy involving a victim–an injury or even death.

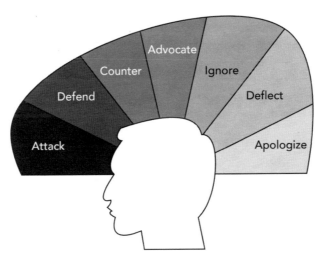

The initial emotional response is caused by adrenaline and cortisol pumping and maybe even endorphins causing your fight response to kick in. Depending on your mood, your typical response style and a host of other factors, your response will lead into one of these standard emotional responses: Attack, Defend, Counterattack, Ignore, Apologize, or Deflect. All these are emotional, and none of them work as well as the seventh response–become their advocate. Let's go through some examples.

Let's assume that a parent has come in, and their child is not being promoted to the next grade. They say, "My child has been retained, and it's your fault." A person that goes on the **attack** will say, "It's because you never get your child to school on time. That's why they're being held back." Or perhaps we really get emotional, and we attack the competency of the child, "Well your child is held back because he isn't very smart." I know as you read this you might not be able to imagine a person saying this to a parent, but it happens!

I also see lots of school employees attempt to **defend** their position. Saying things like, "We just don't have the time to educate our children. We don't have time to provide that extra framework for people with the issues that your child's dealing with." That doesn't come across great, either, does it? No one likes anyone that falls into a defensive posture. So we know that to attack the person is bad. We know that to get in a defensive position is bad.

I'm personally good at the **counterattack**. I love a good counterattack (when I'm emotional and don't care about the long-term negative effects). I can see it when other people counterattack, too. Let's take the parent who comes in and reports their child is being bullied. A counterattack is, "Maybe if you toughened your kid up, they wouldn't get picked on so much." You're pushing the blame onto them. It seems clear that if we want a positive resolution, we should not counterattack.

Oftentimes we **ignore** problems. Think about the times you get a phone call. You'll pick up your phone, and you'll see it, and you can tell it's going to be a stressful situation, and you just don't want to answer the phone. So you simply turn it over and don't answer it. I think we've all done that. I've done it. I say, "I'm just going to ignore this right now. Maybe it'll go away." But it doesn't, right? To ignore the situation often upsets the person more, and then they get even more upset because a vacuum of information will lead the mind to wander.

And worse of all, you know the situation still exists and has not been resolved. So it rolls around in your brain taking up your precious time when you could be doing something more productive.

TIP: Only ignore a problem you are sure will resolve itself naturally.

A lot of people dealing with conflict believe that it'll get better if they just wait it out. Perhaps it will but oftentimes ignoring the problem only makes it worse. I was attempting to think of examples of when waiting benefits me and I have come up with a short list. First, when the problem is not my problem to solve, second if it's not a situation where I can be punished in any manner. Now these situations are difficult to find and I'm not always right, so just make sure you really have the power to ignore a difficult situation that is right in front of you.

Deflection is a fun response to use on your friends when they bring up politics or religion and you are just wanting a nice night. Because after all who wants to argue over dinner. So deflection over small talk can be very useful, but when dealing with real conflicts deflection resolves nothing.

TIP: Next time you're at dinner and someone brings up an uncomfortable topic, just announce in a voice that everyone can hear, "How did Micheal Jackson dance the way he did when he has a glass eye?" Watch the conversation change to people discussing this new topic: Does he have a glass eye? What dance moves? Who is Micheal Jackson? You will be off the bad topic in no time! And just to be clear, Michael Jackson did not have a glass eye, it's a deflection and you just fell for it!

Apologizing is often touted as a great way to deal with conflict. It is nice, but often is not enough and can even make things worse. Now, I'm not saying you can't say you're sorry, but I think you've got to do it in the proper context. Because just rolling over and saying, "I'm sorry. I'm sorry your child's getting bullied. I'm sorry your child's been retained," doesn't really resolve the disruption, does it? It doesn't really fix the problem at hand. It just makes them want to go after your jugular—especially fighters. Nobody wants to hear your apologies until they know that you're empathetic, and you're going to help resolve the issue.

Which brings us to the only correct answer, which is to sell, to **advocate.**

Now, to become a person's advocate, you have to actually want to resolve the issue. Do you want to resolve the bullying? Do you want to resolve the retention issue? I didn't say you must resolve in the person's favor—that you must advocate for their desires. I'm talking about advocating for resolution of the conflict.

This is nuanced. When I'm conducting roleplays, somebody will say, "You said I had to resolve the problem, Brian." Yes. That is what I said, but what I see them doing is resolving it in the person's favor. You can't *not* retain their child. Parents want you to, and you can't. It feels like an impasse, but there is something you can do. You can advocate for the process and why it is what it is, and what can be done in the future to make sure that the child isn't retained again. That feels like a more forward-thinking vision of recreating this situation into a positive one. I know they're going to be upset for a while. Their child's been retained. It stinks. But what can you do to advocate?

Let's take the retention situation. Here's our system that's fair to everyone. We want to be fair to Johnny or Eva or Shamika. Let's assume that little Shamika is being retained. Why is that best for Shamika? It hurts their feelings. I get it. It upsets people. Students want to go on with their classes and graduate on time. An educator's job is to make sure this child is set up for success in life. So, mom, so, dad, the reason the child's being retained is because we're doing everything we can to make sure Shamika is successful in life. Now, that's going to hurt right now. I get it. You're upset. I've been upset. If my child was retained, that would hurt my feelings. I know it bothers people, but long-term we believe that this is the best thing for your child. Here's what we can do to avoid them ever getting retained again. Let's work on a plan together.

Notice in that example, I didn't cave. I didn't just give into them and say, "Shucks, we can't retain them," or "You're stuck. You're getting retained. I don't really care what your feelings are." I took eight or 10, 20 minutes with them. Seems like a long time, but not if they're screaming at everyone for the next year about their child. I explained to them in a selling way why we are doing what we're doing. I'm selling why this problem has occurred. I'm not selling them by telling them I have a deal for them. We're not talking about that kind of selling. We're talking about really advocating for them and being on their team.

When you talk about the seven emotional responses to disruption–that fight or flight. The biological response, let's say, will lead you to one of these, but it will not lead you towards selling. It's not going to lead you to selling because that's a non-emotional response. That requires you to think because your instincts are going to get you to ignore it, to deflect it, to apologize just to get them out of your face. But emotion is not going to elicit this advocate response.

RULE 7

ASSUME POSITIVE INTENT

I use this example a lot, which is let's assume old Brian Stephens is running late, and I do not call my wife. She got dinner ready. Maybe it's her night to do dinner, and I didn't call her. I didn't let her know, and two hours went by. She texted me, and I did not text her back. This is a hypothetical. I would never actually do anything like this. OK, OK, it's probably happened. I didn't call her. I didn't communicate. Now, her brain typically will go in one of two directions, and neither one of them assumes positive intent, such as Brian must be really wrapped up in taking care of an important client. That's awesome. He's taking care of his team, or he's at a food kitchen. He's feeding the homeless, and it ran over. He is such a lovely person that does all this volunteer work. No. That's not the way our brains are designed. We've got to get ourselves ready for something bad that could be going on. We start to get our brains ready for worst-case scenarios.

A lot of women will go to—and I don't know, men don't go to the first one like women do—safety violation. That's the first worry a lot of humans will have. I am late, so I must be dead in a ditch somewhere. A lot of people think that that's a worst-case scenario. Another scenario is I'm out there doing something I ain't supposed to be doing. I'm into mischief. I don't know what that mischief could be, but it could go lots of different ways. I'm with people I'm not supposed to be with, or I'm getting into some sort of trouble.

The human brain is designed to anticipate something bad has happened to be mentally and emotionally prepared to deal with it. That's why the brain will push, oftentimes, to this negative deduction. Now, this is in general. It's funny. I'll give this course, and somebody will say, "I'm always positive. I'm always happy." That's awesome. If you can write a book and teach us all how to do that, I will read it. I will memorize it. I will lock it in my brain because most of us just aren't like that. Once again, we're still trying to set this realistic expectation on how you deal with issues of disruption. To say that you're always happy and always respond–I'd love to meet that person because even people who are positive and proactive get upset from time to time. I've seen them ignore situations. Maybe it happens less frequently, but it happens nonetheless.

Often what many people do, and this is the flight response, too, is to ignore the situation. But when you ignore it, and you don't take that phone call right then, you're going to have to call the person back. That's going to take you more time, isn't it? Also, you're going to be thinking about it. They call. You don't take it. Then your brain starts to develop fear. You didn't answer it because you have some sort of fear. You don't want to be bothered by the situation. Then more fear starts to kick in. False emotions appearing real: FEAR. You start to inflate how bad the situation is going to be. You can inflate how terrible it's going to go. You can start to work out scenarios in your head, and it just takes time. Time is the greatest commodity, the only commodity we really have. To ignore it and to have to put it off and kick the can down the road just means you're going to have to suck up bad energy for too long in your brain. It's going to be tapdancing in your head, and you want to get it out.

RULE 8

PEOPLE VENT, LET THEM

If upset families do not vent to you, they will vent to others. The key is allowing them to vent to you rather than to your team and social media or other parents. We must contain and resolve their issues, and this is tough if we have not heard them!

I know you are busy, but please trust me, you either take an extra few minutes at the start of an issue, or you will take hours later dealing with the fallout. Your goal is you're not trying to rush them out the door. You've got to let them be heard. You want to listen. Maybe you could get them to write it down. Psychologically, it's great to get people to write down their issues. Basically, writing helps the brain shift from the emotional hemisphere to the more logical centers of our brains, slowly diffusing the matter and, thereby, better allowing us to resolve the matter.

For example, If you've ever been upset and really mad, and you write an email, you notice how at the end of the email you're not as upset anymore? It's because you're switching hemispheres, and you're getting those emotions out. If you can get upset parents to write down their thoughts, it'll get them to process more logically. You'll also have your evidence from the parent side recorded in detail. Then you can go get your evidence from the student's records and the teacher, and then you can bring everyone back together in a timely fashion and advocate for the child. Not for what the parent wants in this situation, but for what's best for the child.

TIP: DO NOT tell someone to "Calm Down." Just think of when you have been upset and heard, "Why don't you calm down?" That is the most ineffective way to calm down an emotional person. They're not going to calm down because you tell them to calm down. Really think about the times when people have told you to calm down. You don't want to calm down. You want to go and get them even more, right?

RULE 9
ROLEPLAY

One of the keys to providing a strong plan to recruit and keep your students and embrace fantastic family services is to practice, practice, practice, practice. It's funny. As an old soldier, there's a fundamental way to practice that works, and there are a lot of ways to practice that are just complete and utter wastes of time. People learn differently. There are auditory learners, visual and kinesthetic learners. You can embrace all learning types in one method that will connect all of them if you practice roleplaying.

What I mean by roleplaying is not getting together for Dungeons and Dragons–which I really enjoyed as a kid. I don't know if anybody wants to get a game going again, but give me a call if you're interested. We're also not talking about the kind of roleplay that's a very complex military maneuver. We are talking about roleplaying between two individuals pretending to be roles in a hypothetical workplace disruption–*acting*. This works, but there are some basic components we have to embrace.

The first and foremost thing you must do to ensure effective roleplaying is induce pressure–stress. You have to create artificial stress. When you're dealing with a disruptive situation, or you're dealing with a complex problem, the fight-or-flight mentality will kick in. The stress and anxiety will start to kick in. If you want to be able to deal with that kind of stress in real life by thinking instead of becoming emotionally reactive, and, certainly, if you want your team to do the same, you've got to practice in a similar emotional context. You have to create artificial stress.

When we're conducting roleplays, you have to invoke stress. The first way to do that is you've got to get the people to stand up in front of their peers. They have to be stared at. They have to have people look at them, and that really actually starts to induce a little bit of anxiety and a little bit of pressure. Some people will say, "I love to get in front of an audience. It doesn't bother me." Not true. Some people are less susceptible to the anxiety of public speaking, but it affects us all a little bit. It affects everyone–even great public speakers–when you start to fire unexpected questions at them in front of their peer group. That simulates the same pressure they get in real life but in a safe area where they can practice.

You've got to get them up, and you've got to induce stress. Now, I think it's really vital that you start slowly with this. You don't start to just hammer away at them. It's great to, number one, get permission to give feedback to them. It seems a little weird, but if they don't verbally say, "I would like feedback. I would like to hear what people think," then they're just not ready. You, if you're moderating a roleplay session, have really got to look at those team members around you. If they're really nervous, and they're really shaken up just by getting up, congratulate them. Give them a round of applause and have them go sit back down. That's a great first start.

Remember, we're not trying to break anybody here. We're trying to let them learn all these skills, especially on how to deal with difficult people, in a safe manner. It's got to feel safe to them. As such, let them stand up and experience the mild stress, give them a round of applause and sit them back down. Those who are a little bit more willing and able at that point, do a soft round of roleplaying to start.

Here's how a typical roleplaying exercise should look: You get one of your team members to come up with a situation they may have faced in their work environment. Let's go with a bullying situation because I think you'll see that often, but it could be anything that front desk staff, teachers or principals are dealing with daily. I don't like to prepare scenarios when I facilitate roleplay. Everyone in those sessions already knows what difficult situations arise. They know what they want to practice. It's amazing. When I go around to all these school districts, they have the answers. Once again, the roleplay is just a tactical way to practice it in a safe manner that helps you improve.

Here's how it goes. I play a parent. I am an actor, and I'm playing a parent in this scenario. My child's been bullied. We get a volunteer on our team, and I say, "I want you to pretend to be the front desk person." I approach you with a scenario. Let's say it's 2:30 on a Wednesday. There are other people in the front office. There are teachers coming and going. It's a little hectic, and you're busy, and here it goes.

Then, depending on their ability level and how many times they've practiced, I'm either going to go in kind of soft and let them warm up to the scenario, or I'm going to go in really hard. This next part is key. As the roleplay leader, you don't let the volunteer say, "Here's what I would do." You ask that they actually act it. Acting, I begin the scene by saying, "I reported three times to the teacher that Emily is being bullied in her class, and I haven't got any response from you. I haven't got any response from the assistant principal, the principal. I am blown off at every aspect, and I don't understand what you're doing about it."

OK. We'll pause. That's the start of the roleplay. You just dig in right away with the scenario. Then that person doesn't get to think or respond, and they just have to take it on the chin and act like they're at the front desk. You have to get them to stand up. You can't let them say, "I think I would do this." No. The participants need to just enter the scene as actors because that creates the pressure that we're looking for.

Know this. We are not looking for perfection. Don't look for perfection. We're just practicing. After they get done, literally the first round could take 30 seconds, a minute, tops. Then you go around to the team and give them positive feedback. What did they do right? Make people give them some praise. I don't know if we call the feedback "grows and glows," but I know we're not allowed to say "you stink." Although, that's the way I like to get it, personally. We have to be a little softer out there in the world–warm people up to this practice. I have been practicing roleplay from the military to law school, all the way through. *I'm* ready to be grilled hard, but we have to let everyone work their way up to this level.

Start by reminding volunteers that roleplaying is just practice, and praise what they did well in the scenario. If they seem willing and able, then you can give them a couple helpful hints to improve, but don't overdo that initially. The first few times you practice this, let it roll out smoother. I have failed at this many times. I allowed teammates to go a little too hard at somebody that wasn't quite ready. So be careful. Get some positive feedback. Get some opportunities to grow, and then do another round and do another round. As people get used to this, they're going to start to improve. They have the answers. Your pro tip is really if you free your team up, they know what to do. If you give them the processes and the procedures for how to deal with difficult people, they will respond correctly once they've had lots of practice. They'll get better and better and better over time.

I really encourage schools, in their weekly or biweekly meetings, to do 10 minutes of roleplay with their teams. Say, "Who had a difficult situation this week that they'd like to challenge one of their teammates to roleplay? Come on up. Let's pick somebody in the audience that you want to have some fun with." It's got to be fun, and it's got to be light. It can't be too serious. Inevitably, what's going to happen the first time you do this is they're not going to stand up. They don't want that pressure. They don't want people looking at them. You have to get them up. You have to give them a round of applause and make them feel good, but don't reduce the pressure. Have them go and act out that scenario, and then have some people give some feedback. Then you may want to let another person try the exact same scenario, based on that new information that everybody heard out loud. Celebrate. Celebrate the fact that you are practicing how to be better in a safe space.

Now, this has a great residual effect. Not only will your team feel more confident dealing with tough situations, roleplay builds a better culture with your team because employees know their teammates have their backs. They know that they're practicing together, and people are working together, and they have other people with whom to practice these scenarios. They're going to feel more comfortable and less vulnerable to the world. All too often, they feel isolated when these situations occur in real life. Sometimes during a disruption, teammates in the periphery of the conflict will hear somebody getting upset and run in other directions. Wouldn't it be fun if we all practiced these scenarios, and instead of running from the conflict, someone might come to your aid–someone who had practice dealing with disruption?

You want to make roleplays fun and light. Maybe you give them a round of applause. I don't know if you have any other perks. The person that has the best scenario, and the person that practiced the most becomes teacher of the week or something, and you can send an email out. People like that praise, and it's well-deserved.

I have listed some of the fundamentals to track. First, I want you to be kind, not nice. This is a tricky wicket. Remember, being nice for its own sake can disregard someone's best interest in the long-term. You're not helping them improve. Nice is sweet. It's polite. You have to push politeness aside if you really want people to grow. You've got to get their permission to do that. For those who have given you permission to help by telling you they really want to grow, you can start making them better by being kind to them and giving them scenarios that are tough: scenarios that don't reduce the pressure, but increase pressure in the safe environment. Make it fun.

They have to stand up. I guarantee you. You're going to do this. You're going to make them stand up. You're going to leave for a month and have somebody else do it. You're going to come back in, and they're all going to be sitting down discussing these scenarios, and they're going to be drinking coffee. That isn't roleplay. That does not create artificial stress. That does not create any pressure. It destroys the strategy that's involved. It's too casual.

You've got to make these scenarios as real as possible. Your teammates know their scenarios. They know what's happening every week. You don't have to use names. Don't make fun of anyone on your team. Make the feedback actionable. Keep practicing until you're locked in, and don't look for perfection. Look for little steps, little five, ten percent improvements over time.

You can roleplay just about anything. You can roleplay getting ready to unleash an entirely new program. Let's roleplay what you're going to say to people when they ask questions. You can get your team ready for frequently asked questions. When we do media training and debate, we fire questions at them, and we drill superintendents. We figuratively beat the board members up in a safe space, so in the real world they are ready to handle the media. They are ready to pivot. You can check out those other rules in this book. We get them set up for success, and roleplay, if you're kind and not nice, will set them up for success, will create a better culture, and will let them know you really care about their performance. Go crush it.

TIP:

Rules for Roleplaying at a Glance

- **Be kind, not nice**
- **Get permission to give feedback**
- **Do not reduce the pressure**
- **Make it fun and light**
- **Stand up**
- **Make it as real as possible**
- **Reinforce the positives**
- **Make feedback actionable**
- **Keep practicing until it's locked in**
- **Do not look for perfection**

RULE 10

ALWAYS DEAL WITH THE PERSON HARMED FIRST

After you stop the harm, do not forget about the person that was harmed.[2] They are, and will remain, your top priority.

It's fairly common during a crisis for the people in charge to crawl into their shells and start thinking the world is out to get them. And you know what? It's not unreasonable for them to start thinking about their own future and how the crisis may impact their jobs or their families. However, these selfish priorities get in the way of dealing with the victims appropriately and with compassion. Certainly, a small dose of self-preservation is healthy, but leaders cannot lose sight of the real victims: those actually harmed or disadvantaged as a result of your district's actions, products, or people.

Dealing with victims is especially tough when lawyers and "bean counters" enter the picture. Lawyers are worried that any perceived admission of fault will prove disastrous in a court of law. Bean counters typically worry about short-term profits. Neither seems to worry much about the court of public opinion, switching loyalties, or the long-term harm companies suffer from neglecting injured parties.

The survivors are always more important than the damage to the business. During a crisis, you may have the urge to fight, or ignore the problem, or

___

2 I have debated with myself on the proper term to use for those harmed that people will understand and to which they won't take offense: victim, survivor, person harmed? I have been all three of those people at different stages of my life and I am just not sure which word fits the most situations. I am just going to use them all, hoping you understand my intent.

get wrapped up in the financial costs rather than take care of the victims. But you must remember, your main goal isn't to make the victims disappear; it's to deal with them, resolve the issue, and allow everyone to move forward.

That being said, there is a difference between making a problem go away and finding a permanent remedy. In responding to the immediate consequences, it's easy to lose sight of the need to fix the underlying problem. Consider assigning different people to these two different goals: validating the victims and involving the victims in the process of recovery.

GOAL ONE: VALIDATE THE PERSON HARMED

Victims need confirmation of their pain and suffering from you. If they are not validated, they will go to the government, public groups, or the media to make sure their point is known.

They also need visibility. They need a platform where they can describe their pain. It's best to have the outlet for their energy directed at you and not the press or the government, so, use your team to determine the best platform for your victims to reach out to you. Is it social media? A phone line with real people on the other end to take note of their concerns? Would a well-monitored email address work?

Research your options, come to a consensus, and enact a plan to validate your victims as soon as possible. Give the victims a way to communicate directly to you, and they will be less likely to vent to others.

GOAL TWO: INVOLVE THE ONE HARMED
IN THE PROCESS OF RECOVERY

Actively engaging with the harmed/victim will diminish the crisis. Victim participation in the resolution helps everyone recover more quickly. If you caused the problem, your engagement with the victims can change the tone of the discussion in a positive, respectful way that leads to mitigation and resolution.

Once you have validated and engaged the victims, don't forget that it's an ongoing process. They need to be kept in the loop with appropriate information in a timely manner. If you care about the victims and do things that show you care, your crisis will be easier to manage.

RULE 11
DISCOVER THE REAL ISSUE

This last rule in dealing with difficult people is what I would almost consider a PhD level course on how to identify and cure the unsaid or unspoken issue at hand. Let me tell you a story about why we started teaching on this particular front and how many people, when they're dealing with conflict or a difficult person, attempt to cure the conflict as quickly as possible, so they can move on with their lives. I understand this. I understand the fight-or-flight mentality kicks in, and you really want to avoid situations of stress. If you can resolve it quickly, why wouldn't you? But often we attempt to solve an issue very quickly, but we misidentify the person's real pain point.

I got a call from a client who was confused because they thought that they had handled the issue perfectly. They thought they had handled it very well, and they couldn't understand why the caregiver, the parent in this case, was still very upset. It was time for the year-end surveys to be distributed to all the parents, so the school could get their views. They'd fill out 10 to 20 questions, and at the end of that survey, they would put a results package together and send it out to everybody.

The survey had been out for about two weeks, and the district had emailed it twice. They'd even sent a text message telling parents to look for the email and check their spam folders. They were not done getting the results. People still had two more weeks left to fill out and submit the surveys. A parent called the communications department for the school district. They were large enough to have at least a small communications department. The head of that department heard the phone call that one of their team members was having with this parent, and the parent was very upset they were not given the survey.

The communications director said, "I can handle this call. I know exactly what to do. I'm going to become their advocate. I've listened to Brian." I'm sure that's not what they thought, but they certainly thought that they could become the parent's advocate, and they could resolve this problem in short order. They took the phone and said, "This is not a big deal. I can send you the survey right now. You didn't get the email, but we can get it to you now. Your results will be included with everyone else." They got off the phone, but then the parent proceeded to go on social media. They showed up to PTA meetings over the course of the next few weeks. The person went crazy. They even went so far as to show up to the board talking about how disrespectful the school system is and how incompetent. They kept using the word *incompetent*.

The communications director called me and said, "I don't know why this person is so upset. I solved their problem." That's when we began to sit down and really dissect what the real issue was. Now, the parent didn't say what the real issue was. They said the issue was they didn't get a chance to fill out the survey. The solution in the school's mind was to simply give the parent the survey. That's not what the real issue was. The real issue was that the parent felt left out. They felt as if no one cared to hear their opinion.

They felt like they were being excluded, and that emotional response to being left out is primal in nature. I don't want to be left out. I do not want to be forsaken. I do not want to be ditched. I do not want to be forgotten. Think about the case in which all your friends go to a dinner, and you show up, and they're all eating, but you didn't know anything about it. They go, "We sent you an email." "I didn't get the email. Nobody told me. You guys didn't care enough to make sure that I was actually here. You sent me one email, but you didn't really care about having me at this dinner."

That's exactly how this parent felt. They felt as if the school didn't care enough to get their opinion. So we did something really simple. We identified the correct issue, and then the communications director called the parent up and said, "I think that the issue for which I failed you (how I wasn't your advocate) is in not listening to you. That is really awful of us, and I do want to make sure you're heard. I do want to make sure we get your opinion. Let's find out why that email didn't go through. I want to make sure you get all my emails. I want to make sure you get all my text messages. Let's really sit down and figure that out."

Now, what they discovered was that the person had gotten the emails. That's the funny thing about all this. The person had gotten the emails. They missed them, or they went to a spam folder. We couldn't exactly get what the issue was, but they had opened the email. It was sent to their box, but they didn't feel special. As such, fighting about whether or not the person did or didn't get the email did not resolve the problem and, in this case, created a customer who didn't feel loved and cared for. All the communications department had to do was to say, "We care about your feelings, and we do want to be heard, so let's make sure we get this resolved so that you're heard." That was the real issue.

I'm not saying discovering the real issue is easy. It is often wrapped up in the subconscious. It is often wrapped up in cloak-and-dagger issues. Often, the harmed person doesn't even know what the real issue is, so how in the world are you supposed to identify it? It takes time, and it takes practice. I would get you to step back, attempt to empathize with them, and say, they're complaining about this, but what are their emotions right now? What are they really upset about? The more and more you work on that, the more I think you'll begin to identify the real issue, and the quicker you'll get to an actual solution that resolves the conflict in a timely fashion and lets everyone get on with their lives and training the children.

SECTION VI:

RULES FOR RECRUITING

In many ways, the rules on "how to recruit students" demands its own book. After all, there is no reason for us to worry about great customer service if we don't have any students. But it's sort of like the chicken and egg–which comes first? I thought long and hard and actually started to write all the rules for recruiting students, then I did a 90-degree turn to address how to deal with difficult people. Then I went back to giving the fundamentals of marketing and running great campaigns to recruit students because school districts must first increase their budgets to gain more resources to train their people.

Frankly, I was going out of my mind trying to figure out which direction to go. Then I sat back, attempting to calm down, which if you met me you will understand is a Herculean effort. I met with our teams assigned to help with training and those assigned to recruit students. I brought in the team that works for districts to keep students from being recruited away from the district. Through all this, I learned one fundamental truth–it all goes together.

I would like to keep this simple and have a clear lesson in this book that is only about recruiting or keeping it just to training, but humans pick schools and stay with schools for all sorts of reasons. And if you begin building an outstanding school, you will begin to see that we have a stool with many legs. One leg represents great education (you are doing that, so you don't need me), and the other legs represent keeping students, obtaining new students, overall reputation in the community, having a well trained team and the list goes on.

Based on my team's comments and our experiences around the nation, I decided to keep this book focused on the main thing: increasing your student population! This means I needed rules on customer service, recruiting, reputation building and whatever else I thought was important because after all I'm the moron who started writing this book, and I simply can't figure out a way to do it better! So below are some rules I think will benefit you.

RULE 1

WINNING DESPITE DISADVANTAGES

I travel the country, teaching people how to use strategic and tactical best practices to recruit students back to public schools. One thing is absolutely clear. We are at a complete disadvantage. The reason why we're at a disadvantage is because traditional public schools just do not have the same marketing and sales budgets as competitors.

For hundreds of years, traditional public schools simply had to teach children how to become successful. They never had to think about recruiting and marketing and all the sales tactics to get someone to make a buying choice to pick their school over another school. The world has changed rapidly, and with the advent of massive competition throughout the United States, they are simply outflanking us when it comes to pushing more and more resources towards their marketing arm.

I think a lot about hamburgers when it comes to this disadvantage. Take McDonald's, for instance: They certainly don't sell the best hamburger, at least in my opinion. Frankly, I have never heard anyone's opinion that McDonald's makes the best hamburger, but they certainly do *sell* the most hamburgers. They sell the most hamburgers because they market and sell their hamburgers constantly.

We'll take this analogy towards public education. We have the best hamburger. Traditional public schools offer the best service for our children, in my opinion. They provide the best education to the greatest number of people, and they do it all with a set budget and set resources. Our competitors, however, have a larger marketing budget, larger sales bucket, and while I don't think they have more rigorous academics than we do, they certainly do have a better marketing arm.

Despite the disadvantage, I still believe that we can win, and I've seen it happen over and over again. I've seen traditional public schools use best practices and simply slightly increase their recruiting arm, and then they outflank and do indeed beat their competition.

> **TIP:** You do not have to compete toe-to-toe with the same resources as your competition. Just five percent improvement in the way that you're recruiting will create massive positive effects for your school district.

RULE 2
KNOW YOUR TARGETS

In marketing and advertising there's an old adage that says, half of our advertising dollars are useless; we just don't know which half. Frankly, with the limited resources public schools have to recruit and market to new students, we have to do better than old advertising techniques.

There are more marketing and sales vehicles that can be better utilized than traditional advertising, but first and foremost, you have to know your targets. Primarily this means we need to limit our marketing tactics to what speaks to a specific audience. Limiting can start based on geographical region. Marketing can be narrowly tailored toward students who have left within the last three years, or to new families who have entered the community, or to families who meet the socioeconomic status of the type of students that reach particular schools. There are many ways to narrow down the particular targets and parents that you want to go after to recruit.

In general, if you're not narrowly tailored, you're trying to talk to everyone. And if you're trying to talk to everyone, you're actually going to talk to no one. Pick your targets, and go with the narrowest target first. Widen the scope of your target audience as you go.

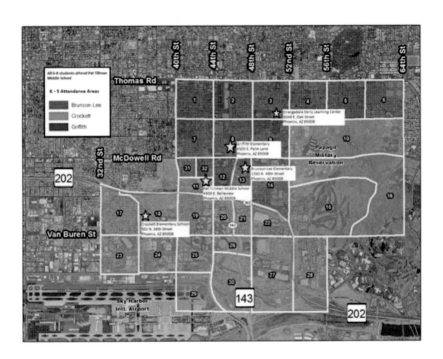

In general, it makes sense to start narrowing the target audience of your marketing to a geographic region. Speaking to the needs of a limited group increases the efficacy of your messaging.

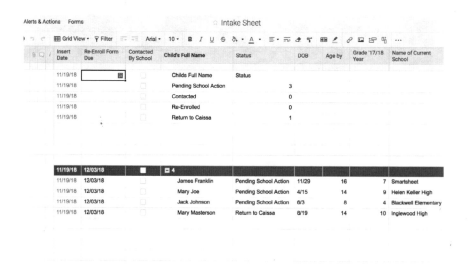

Alerts & Actions   Forms

In the case of public schools, recruitment needs can be sorted to create even more specific target audiences for marketing, such as families who've left the district within set time frames.

RULE 3

DON'T DO WHAT YOU CAN'T DO

I preach about this often. The one thing that we're asking you to do is a 5, 10, 15, 20 percent improvement in your enrollment and your recruitment processes. That will go a long way. That's just picking up low-hanging fruit. What happens all too often is people don't know how to say no to a good idea. A pro tip for you right now is to learn how to say no to really good ideas. You're going to get so many ideas about how to recruit and how to keep students and how to engage students. We have to have a TikTok; we have to have Instagram; we have to have Facebook; we have to have whatever the latest social media construct; we have to send e-blasts; we have to send text messages; we have to do billboards; and we need ... It goes on and on.

I promise you, there's more than anyone could possibly do in the recruitment space. If you had unlimited resources and unlimited time, and it was all infinite, you still couldn't do it all. It gets overwhelming. Let me give you one real-world example that I used to see. It's outside the school space, but I do think it's telling. We used to represent a lot of homeowners' associations. I, as a young lawyer, did. It was interesting that a homeowners' association would get together, and some volunteers would come together with all great intent. They were motivated. They were excited about building up their community and getting it cleaned up, and they would start a newsletter. They would commit to sending out a newsletter once a quarter.

It was always done by a volunteer, and inevitably, you know exactly what happened, it stopped. Or they miss a quarter, and then they'd come back and do another one, and then they'd miss a couple years, a couple months, and then the person that was in charge of doing it moved, and then nobody else picked it up for a year. Then what would happen is the homeowners' association was getting consistent dues from everybody before the newsletter. In some areas of the country, homeowners' associations have required dues, and in some it's voluntary, but this was in volunteer areas. Even when you're required to give dues, when they stopped sending out the newsletter, everyone thought the homeowners' association dissolved, so they'd stop paying their dues. Then they'd have to effect this massive effort to reinvigorate people and get them to send homeowners' association dues. All of this because people thought the group had gone away.

I'm letting you know, this didn't happen in one group. This happened over and over and over again. Then I saw it with PTA and parent-teacher organizations, PTOs. They would get so juiced up that they were going to really bring all these families together, and they were going to do a great job, and they said, "We're going to do these 25 awesome things." Maybe they did 12 awesome things, but they committed and promised to do all these other things, and then somebody moved, or the child graded up, and that parent left; the person driving the ship moved on, and the organization fell apart.

When we have suggested and gotten people to work with us, instead of doing 25 things or committing to doing 25 things, or committing to do 12 things, we try to encourage clients to commit to doing three. Just three really well. Let the rest of it go. Say no to all those good ideas. TikTok would be great. Instagram would be great, but we don't have the resources, and we don't have the time necessary to really do those in a consistent pattern over and over again, and that's really what great communication takes. That's really where you have to establish a baseline on how you're going to connect and engage with your families. I'm talking about not just the families you're trying to recruit, but also the ones that you want to keep.

Sometimes we say we're going to send out a weekly email, and then we miss a couple weeks. You're busy teaching the babies, and I think that's your job. I'm telling you. People hear this and think, "But I could do it all. I have to do it all. This is important, Brian." It is, but you have to be realistic. It's better to say we're not going to do a great job on doing 25 things, so let's just do a consistent solid job on three. Then we can add a fourth and fifth later on, once we've established that we can do those really, really well. People try to eat the entire elephant, the entire cake, all at one time, and it gets overwhelming.

> **TIP: If you try and do it all at once, you will accomplish nothing. You can do it all, just not all at once.**

I think about another example. I think about those marquee signs out in front of schools. You'll hear me talk about this. Often, they're out of date. We're so excited about the winter holidays coming, and it's still up in mid-February. The students are already back, but no one's taken the time, had the time, to go out there and adjust what the lettering says on those signs in front of some of your schools. Get rid of them. Somebody goes, "But aren't they a good idea?" Yes. They are a good idea *if* you utilize them, if you utilize them *correctly*. What destroys your reputation is out of date material that you just don't have the time and resources to keep up. If you can't keep the sign up to date, own it. Say, "We're too busy educating your children to keep this sign up to date." That's kind of like an evergreen message, right? It's funny, and it also lets them know that you know what your primary job is, which is to educate the babies, not to keep the sign updated.

That's what I mean. People who try to seek perfection in all this, one: It can't happen. It's never going to happen. You need to accept that, and you need to give yourself a break. Just give your team a break and say, we're not going to do that well. Our job is to train the children, not keep signs updated, not to do TikTok and Instagram. It would all be great, but this is our primary job. Now let's decide what we can do consistently on the communications front, and know what you can't do right now, and just accept it. It's not a big deal. People put so much pressure on themselves to do everything that oftentimes it all falls apart.

I think a lot about websites on this front, too. What happens with a lot of websites is, one: You have a certain Americans with Disabilities Act (ADA) requirements. You've got to meet all those. I understand that. Two: You get designers with great intentions but who absolutely put too many widgets on the website, and no one can actually keep them up to date long-term.

I know a lot of you, because of ADA, are required to have calendars, but I think it's appropriate to say, "We're going to put the things that we have the time and are legally required to put on the calendar, but we don't have a full-time person just to update every little thing that's going on in our school. If you really want to know what's going on in our school, please go to our Facebook page. That's where we update." There can be too many drop-down menus, and then people keep adding to the website. Then what you'll find is broken links because no one updates or checks them. It's kind of like having that sign in front of your building that's up to date.

A new family is considering enrolling in your school. They go to your website, and what they see are broken links, a lot of spaces that have current news, and it's completely blank, and it's been blank for months and years. On this one, they had really good contact information, but you'll see out-of-date contact information. You'll see a principal that's no longer the principal on the website. It just makes people think that you're not squared away, and that you're not tight. Nobody really thinks, "They're so busy educating the children that they're not keeping this website up." You have to own that. Maybe a disclaimer. We do our best job to keep this website up to date, but know this, we are too busy educating your babies, and all of our resources go to educating our students, not keeping this website up to date, so please excuse typos. Please excuse the out-of-date content.

I think that that creates a narrative and a message that you are focused on your main and most important job, and it's also letting go of the stress of trying to make a perfect website. I've never seen one. I've never seen one in or out of schools. Even companies that have multibillion-dollar marketing budgets can have websites can have trainwreck websites. You just have to let it go. I'm going to continue to give disclaimers on this because I get beat up so many times about this. If you can do it all, awesome. Do it all. I love it. I love it. I ain't never seen it, and I'd love to see it. So if you've got it so squared away, let go.

What you can and what you can't do well applies to school tours. I was training a district on giving better tours. I'm going to use that word "better" because I don't ever want perfect to be the enemy of doing better, but all too often, people let perfect be the enemy of better. They can't be perfect, so they just do nothing. They got really offended that I said their tours aren't as good as their competition. They got really upset. "We give great tours." I go, you do, but it's still not as good as the competition. Then the true emotion came out, the real emotion. The real issue came out, which was "We don't have the resources, and we're at a disadvantage to provide these great caliber first-rate tours to new families." I said, "I know. I'm just asking you to do 5-8 percent better than what you did last year." Not 100 percent.

I don't even want you to give a tour as good as the competition. I think if you're giving perfect tours and perfect websites and perfect social media, you're probably not doing your job of educating the children. I want you to stay focused on that. I think that that is your competitive advantage in traditional public schools. You train the children better.

I just want a little bit of improvement in reputation building, recruitment and keeping your students. People get so upset that they can't do it all, and they feel trapped, so they don't want to recognize they can just do a little bit better. What I'm going to encourage you to do is decide what you can do a little bit better and pick that, and learn to say no. I'm going to keep saying it. Learn to say no to the things you can't do. That's OK. It's OK.

The next big area of knowing what you can do and can't do is general reputation issues. It's easy to get overwhelmed by general media and community meetings. I don't really know what the answer is on what you can do and what you can't do on building a great reputation, but I'll give you one pro tip: Emails. Emails are consistent. They're easy to generate. They are cost effective. I know we all get too many of them, but in the 21st Century, we keep our email addresses longer than we keep our home addresses. It's interesting. You even change cell phone numbers now, sometimes more often than you change your email addresses. They hold, and if it's a good powerful subject line from somebody a recipient knows, like their children's school, they will look at it. They will read it. You can do it consistently over time, and that will build your reputation.

As far as going on media tours, I think when you have big issues, you ought to do it. I think when you have something to really promote, you should do it. New buildings, a number one teacher in the state, scholarships you got for your students or a new program—you need to exercise those. Accept that you're not going to do that consistently throughout the year. I see some districts worry so much about the media they forget that the media is not who they're attempting to communicate with. The media is a vehicle to communicate to prospective families and their current families. It's a vehicle. But email is a vehicle, also.

Just pick the ones you can do really great. I think what you'll find out is that you'll do it better. You'll be consistent. You'll own what you can do, and you'll end up doing a better job in general. You'll also have more—I'm going to steal this from the Miami-Dade County School District: Joy is one of their prospects. Your team will have more joy because what you're providing them is a realistic achievable goal of what they can do and not do. I hope this helps. Let's destroy some of those barriers to entry and recognize that you can do what you can do, and it's OK to not do what you can't.

RULE 4
ONE-PAGERS

Simple marketing pieces are often referred to by many names, such as collateral, brochures, one-pagers, marketing pieces, infographs and probably names of which I've never heard. The general concept is the same: a document to give to potential families making a buying decision. A one-pager is something they hold onto and glance at to reinforce your school's competitive advantages. I prefer to use the term one-pager, even though the document may be two-sided or trifold, may have beautiful images, or a lot of words, because I believe that the term one-pager best captures what I've seen work the best. A simple, short, concise document that is cheap to produce and easy to adjust.

There are two major problems with marketing pieces that have to go to a professional print house, need experienced graphic designers or require bureaucratic approvals: 1. They never get done or 2. They become outdated and never updated with information like the name of the current principal. One-pagers, on the other hand, are typically documents that can be done quickly, in-house, with local printers and can be adjusted and fixed by just about anyone. This speed is the key to making sure that there's a document in the hand of every potential parent and caregiver when they leave your school as they're beginning to make their buying decision.

Now, this may be the one rule in this book that doesn't go along with the premise that you can read every rule individually and get something out of it. Simply realizing that every school in your district needs a one-pager to hand out to parents is, alone, a pretty good rule. But in order to make that one-pager stand out and have power and impact, you probably should go and read the rules on 321 messaging, which will allow you to have three powerful messages in your document. That's it. One will certainly be around the success of the child, one about safety and one about some other competitive advantage that your school has. You should also read the rule on making the ask because the document should in some place make the ask to have them enroll. Certainly, include powerful pictures of children. Faces and images are always powerful things. I just would caution you not to try to make a perfect document. Instead, make a document that has your competitive advantages, and one that is ready to hand out immediately.

> **TIP:** Make sure these documents are being used. All too often, we find that a communications team or a front desk staff member will make a really great one-pager, and then never hand it out. They think that these documents become their own little fiefdoms. They love to have them stacked and organized. The real key to these documents is to burn them up—to use them as quickly as possible and print more. Printing cost is cheap compared to the value of gaining new students.

RULE 5

MAKE THE ASK

If you talk to anybody who does professional fundraising for nonprofits, charities, even political campaigns, there's one critical rule that gets people to give more than any other: They make the ask.

For some reason, in American culture it's very difficult for somebody to ask for what they want. We all act like we're strong, direct people, but when it comes to asking for money or for a purchasing decision, we all get a little soft in the knees, and we dance around the issue.

A great example of this issue exists in political campaigns, where political candidates will call up someone from whom they need money, and they'll talk to them about their candidacy, and they'll explain who they are as a person. Then they say, "I'd really love your support." The person will reply, "Absolutely." They get off the phone, and later, the candidate wonders why they never got any money. The reason: because they didn't say, I need $1,600.

When we say "make the ask" in the student recruitment category, we mean, ask them to enroll. You can give them a great tour. You can give a great one-pager. You can give them all of your fantastic messaging points, but if you don't cultivate that by asking them to actually enroll, you're leaving a lot of latitude for the competition to make a stronger ask and to get them. People *want* to be asked for their support.

Let me give you one additional example based on political races. How a person votes is a very personal decision, and how a parent chooses a school is also a very personal decision–perhaps even more so. In political campaigns there are those called super voters, people who never miss an election. They're very valuable because they're going to vote, and you want them to vote for you. You'll see candidates who will go out there and talk to super voters endlessly, and then if you ask the super voter who they voted for, they say, "I didn't vote for that person." You go, "Why not? You spent an hour with them. They talked to you. They told you all of their great reasons." They go, "They never asked me to vote for them. I expect to be asked."

Parents expect to be asked. Please, on your enrollment forms, on your one-pagers, on your website, make the ask. During tours that you give of the school, at the end, ask them to enroll. This is a game changer when it comes to recruiting students, and I can't emphasize this point enough.

TIP: Don't imply an ask, use direct, concrete words.

RULE 6
VIP TOURS

It's funny how some schools spend a lot of time really thinking about how to give a tour to a prospective parent, yet other schools simply deal with whoever walks in the door with whichever employee is available. Your competition, however, is providing first class tours. Yes, they have more resources. Yes, public schools are at a disadvantage. You can't do giveaways. You can't open up a red carpet for them, but what you can do is press your school's selling points.

One of the silly things that happens during tours is people always want to highlight the negative. It's kind of baked into our genetic code. People focus on the negative instead of the positive. You've got to really stop your teammates from giving tours highlighting things that they don't like.

For instance, we've secret shopped at hundreds of schools over the years, and a typical comment from school staff tour guides might be, "Ignore the dirty carpet. Ignore the cobwebs on the ceiling." I'll say, "I didn't even notice the cobwebs. I didn't even notice the dirty carpet until you pointed it out." People are highlighting the wrong things. What I'm suggesting is to get staff to highlight the positives of the school. Then, during the tour, ask parents questions about what they want for their children. Focus on that, and at the end, make the ask. (See the rule right above.)

If you start to produce tours that are *slightly* better than you did before, you'll see positive returns. Do not expect a massive readjustment with the limited resources you have. I'm just saying be a little bit more conscious about how you roll out those first impressions.

We get a little bit more into first impressions in the secret shopping rules, so you might want to refer to that to learn more about what parents are looking for during their shopping experiences.

> **TIP:** Ask the parents questions to allow you to streamline the tour with what they want, not what you want to talk about. Give them the one-pager, and focus on your positives, not your negatives. Finally, make the ask.

RULE 7
GRASSROOTS EFFORTS

One of the key components that we found to be very effective in recruiting students is good old-fashioned grassroots efforts. Once you've established exactly who your targets are–and remember, that's got to be as narrow as you can possibly make it–then you've got to figure out how to reach them. Things like billboards, radio ads, TV ads, that's more akin to a large "air campaign" meant to hit many people at once. Typically, public schools don't have a budget high enough to hit everyone in a given community. It's just too costly, and you don't get high enough return on investment.

What we found much more efficient is increasing tactics in a ground campaign. For example, once you have your target list, you call them. You get on the phone and ask them to enroll. You share those 321 messaging points, and you talk to them about why your school rocks. You might even go door-to-door, presenting those exact same things, the 3-2-1 message points. You give them those one-pagers. It's boots on the ground that make a big difference.

At CaissaK12, we send teams to daycares and preschools–where much of your competition is going to recruit students–because once you get a preschooler or kindergartener to enroll, that family may stay with your district for years. I know it's crass to talk about a student having a monetary value, but they do have monetary values. I think nationwide it's somewhere between $7,000-$8,000 per student. If you keep that student year after year, that's a compounding effect. The younger you get those students enrolled, the better. As such, you go to events. You have trained people who make the ask going door-to-door, going to daycares, going to supermarkets, going to festivals. That takes a Herculean effort.

Now, one caveat to this and a pro tip for you is not to ask your teachers and principals and staff to do this. It's not because they wouldn't be good at it.

It's not what they were meant to do. They were meant to teach the children, and that's what they do well. Every single time we've attempted to get teachers or principals to go door-to-door or make phone calls, it gets them very off the track of their primary mission in life, which is to train the children–a taxing and important job. Principals, staff and teachers are critical to keep your students, but for recruiting elements, it's a little outside of their day-to-day activities. It adds too much pressure, and, frankly, it's not what they're trained to do. You need a trained team to conduct grassroot efforts. Through this approach, we've seen much higher returns on investment for those hours.

SECTION V:

THE COMPETITION

It's a competitive landscape out there, and that's cool. I'm an American. In America, you want to compete. You have Coke, and you have Pepsi. You have McDonald's, and you have Burger King. Competition is good for the soul, but you have to know what the competition is doing and how they're selling to your families–especially when it comes to keeping your students. If they're marketing heavy, and they're saying things to get your students to move from your school to their charter school, homeschool or private school, then it impacts how much money you have left to educate the kids that you have remaining. In almost every district across the United States, your budget is completely dependent on the number of students you have showing up, so if you lose a student, you lose all the money that goes with them. I want you to know, so you can start thinking about what you can do to effectively counter, but also how you can sell yourself, how you can market yourself.

Now, one important thing about marketing. You're stuck with the truth. Not every competitor is. Let's talk about advertising. Some of us might recall a popular fast-food chain ad featuring the slogan "Where's the beef?" If you're not familiar with this ad, it happened quite a while ago. McDonald's was the number one fast food franchise in the United States. Burger King was number two, and a little girl with red pigtails, Wendy's, was a distant third. Wendy's decided that it was going to become number two. It wasn't going to beat McDonald's any time soon, but it could probably beat Burger King.

The marketing team at Wendy's started an ad campaign: You see the burger right here, little burger on a big bun? "Where's the beef?" The entire ad campaign was making fun of Burger King for not having enough meat in their hamburgers. People believed that Wendy's had bigger, meatier hamburgers than Burger King. Was it true? Did Wendy's actually have more meat than Burger King? Not necessarily. But it's marketing, it's advertising.

Take Burger King, McDonald's, and Wendy's, and other fast food places like Taco Bell now, and think about that as the school competition. You have traditional public schools. That's who we represent here at CaissaK12. Then you have charter schools, homeschools and private schools. They're your competition. Kids not showing up to any school at all is also a problem.

Ads don't have to be true, and your competition knows this. I know that *you're* subjected to the truth. I get it, but your competition isn't always. I'm not going to claim all competitors are deceptive, but some are. This is important for you to know because you may be talking to your parents one day, and they might show you advertising for another district that's going to make it look like your school isn't rigorous or isn't safe enough. It's important that you understand the competition's marketing strategies. Through our national parent survey, we've learned there are two main drivers that parents value when considering a school or district. One: Will my babies be safe? Two: Will they move out of my house? At least, that's the way I think about it. Some parents would say, will my child be successful at whatever their given trade or education level is? Will they be successful?

TIP: All images referenced can be seen in an art spread at the end of this section.

Your competition knows this, also, and you're going to see much of the advertising they produce highlights safety and the future. This first competitor marketing image pictured below says, delivering high-quality education, no matter what zip code. What they're implying is that they don't care where your child comes from. By law, public schools have to take everybody, yet we know that most competitors want your best and your brightest. So this ad is a little false. It's implying that you, public school employee, don't care about every zip code. Lights and bells should be going off right now, letting you know that that's not true.

The next competitor marketing image gets it because of the polling data we know they know. They're advertising that the difference they provide in education is your child's success. They're implying that they're different from private schools, online schools or whomever their competition is because they're going to ensure your child is successful. What? Children can be successful going to all kinds of different schools. But they're advertising. They're leaning into something their targets, their parents, really want and demand, which is a successful child.

This next competitor ad is cute. Build your own school. Personalized, customized. They're not laying bricks and literally building a school. It's advertising. Maybe they're letting the kids pick some courses, which, by the way, a lot of traditional public schools offer, too. But it's a good selling point. If you don't have the ability to customize the curriculum at certain grades, you don't advertise that. Figure out what you're good at and highlight that.

This next competitor ad plays right into the safety facet of the national parent survey. "Teen busted at Liberty High School with more than $3,000 worth of cocaine." Look at this. They literally say it to you. They're not hyperbolic. They're not figurative. They are literal. Why worry about this type of student at your school? Come to us because we don't have any bad children. None of our children would do drugs or drink alcohol. Nobody would.

I got to tell you, we had a daughter who was in private schools for awhile, and if you want to know who's got drugs, it's often the kids with money. But the truth is that everyone has access to drugs. Everyone has access to alcohol. I'm not saying that one school has more, but parents shopping for a school might not know or stop to think about that. This competitor doesn't have any scientific proof to prove that there are fewer drugs at their school versus another school. They don't have any data. They took an article and drilled it into a parent's emotional state because they know emotions are why we make decisions most of the time.

When we're making a buying decision, many of us are often led by emotions first and use facts to justify our emotional decisions. Choosing a school, type of schooling or district is a buying decision for parents. It's a critical buying decision. It's important to them. They're picking a school for at least the next year for their babies, so it's important. If something gets their emotions to believe that your school is unsafe, they will pick a different school. If they believe that you're safe, they may pick you, and then they'll use facts to justify the emotional response. But this charter school does not have any data in a courtroom–just the court of public opinion–to prove their school is more safe than others, pound for pound, based on population sizes.

Now look at this other ad. This one is leaning into success. "Our chess players are always a few moves ahead," implying they're just a little bit better than their competition. It's important that you know your competition understands their targets and what drives them. If you're not speaking to your families' emotional states, know that somebody else will. If you're not answering their questions, if you're not leaning into their fears and their concerns, a competitor will address that.

Let's get back to that safety issue. In the next ad, you'll see reasons why you should homeschool. They write that a homeschooled child will get to keep their innocence, which really leans into that safety issue again. They're still saying that your child will be safe–innocent and protected. I think keeping a child's innocence is probably a competitive advantage of homeschooling. I'm not saying all homeschools do this, but I can see a situation where if you never let your child go out; you don't let them see TV; you don't let them see the Internet; you make them study reading, writing, and arithmetic and take tests that you create; and you block out the outside world, then you can absolutely keep them innocent for as long as you have them.

Now, I think that's a competitive advantage of homeschools. I don't think that a public school could ever claim that as its space. It's funny. One of the things that you always know in business is you're looking for what your competitive advantage is. What makes you special? What makes you unique? Innocence, if that's the thing that parents want–I don't want that for my child, but I can see why some parents would want that–you got to give that to homeschools. They're going to keep their innocence forever and ever, I guess. I want my child to be ready for the real world. I want her to have a little street smarts. I want her to have a little common sense. I want her to be in a problem-solving mood. I want her to wrestle with tough situations while I can guide and prepare her before I lose her off to college. I believe public schools can make this preparation possible.

What's your competitive advantage? Somebody's reading this and going, "That's not up to me. That's up to the district or the principal." But if you're a teacher or if you're a front desk worker, those are the most vital spots. Those are critical. You absolutely know what makes your individual school special. You know what makes your classroom unique and cool and better than the competition. Maybe the classroom size is a little bit bigger than some of the competitor schools. That may be true, and you know that's not the competitive advantage; however, maybe you have access to great computer labs. Maybe you have an unbelievable sports program, which a lot of charter schools and homeschools don't necessarily have. Maybe you can help develop a well-rounded student–for those who see that as a competitive advantage.

We were working with a district down in Texas who said, "We don't have a competitive advantage, Brian. We're not special. We're just run of the mill, small district, few thousand students. There's just nothing unique." I was like, "Let's break that down. I don't know if you've wrestled with that problem long enough." We sat down. I have to admit. We went down, and it's a couple hours north of Dallas. Its location was remote: deserts and cacti. It was pretty, but there wasn't much out there. I talked to them on the phone a couple times. I decided to pop over. I spent all morning with the superintendent and two other people who worked there in the office. So there's four of us, and we're sitting around. I've got to admit, I could not figure out what their competitive advantage was. I did not know what made them unique. I did not know what made them cool. There was a private school recruiting many wealthy families with assets for tutoring toward good test scores. There was a neighboring district that was bigger and had a better sports program and a better band program. Band, extracurricular activities and arts absolutely can be competitive advantages.

I decided to go look at a school. Two things smashed me in the face. I couldn't believe that they didn't want to talk about them. I encountered the first one when I walked up and saw drones flying. I said, "You got some drone coverage." They replied, "We start to give our young children, even in elementary school, access to learning about drones and that kind of technology. We have a high school class that students can take about manning drones because we have all these big Amazon warehouses and other companies that need drones. So we're starting to work on training them." I'm like, "Guys, that's a really cool program. How come you're not telling everybody about it?" They said, "We didn't know it was a competitive advantage. We didn't know that it was special." I go, "It's so special. It's so unique, and it's very cool."

This is not just about saying, "We have a drone program." No. It's also about the fact that this was a very small district where everyone knows everyone. This was a small district with cutting-edge technology being considered and implemented. This was one example of cutting-edge training and teaching given to students, which also implies the district would continue paying attention to the future and what's next. So if you were working for this district, you might say, "We're always looking for new opportunities for our children, and here's one awesome example. Drone practice, drone skills." I saw another district in Arizona, doing this drone stuff. It was cool, but the Arizona district was only allowing STEM people to do it because they didn't have as much of the technology to go around. This superintendent in Texas got drones donated to the school. It showed that they were forward thinking.

The second thing I noticed upon walking into the elementary school, is that it was the most bright, vibrant place, but not because they had a new building. You could tell that these teachers were totally enveloped in showcasing why their students are awesome, and it was all over the walls. I said, "Your next competitive advantage is to invite people for a tour. If they come and walk around this building, they will pick you over the competition because I walked around their buildings, too. They just didn't have the energy you had." The energy for success, the energy to make these children stars, were absolutely competitive advantages.

This next marketing tactic from the competition is a main driver, and charter schools have this one figured out. Unfortunately, public schools do not, and private schools are kind of a mix. Some private schools do really well, and some just do it terribly. Charter schools have got the main driver toward getting parents to make a buying decision: They ask. They ask the parents to enroll. They ask the parents to stay.

Now, I know. I know. You're thinking, "Brian, we give them grades. We tell them we love them. We say, 'I can't wait to see you next year.'" But it's not the same thing.

The science about making the ask started with a specific model that's been translated into all these other universes and tested frequently. In political campaigns, there's a person called a super voter. They never miss an election. If there's an election for dog catcher, they're there. If it's a primary, a general, it doesn't matter. They always show up and vote. They're special in campaigns because if you can identify someone who's absolutely going to vote, you should talk to them and convince them to vote for you rather than trying to convince people who don't vote at all to start. The latter is more work because you have to talk them into voting, and then you have to talk them into voting for you or your cause.

These super voters are really important. They're often engaged at exit polls: "Why'd you vote for so-and-so?" And often the super voters reply, "Because they asked." People started doing focus groups on this going all the way back into the 1950s and 1960s. The focus groups asked, "Why is the ask so important to you?" Super voters replied, "Because it's my vote, and if you don't want it, I'm not going to give it to you."

Now, I'm paraphrasing. But generally, the response could be construed as petty. They had candidates or an issue campaign that would talk to this person, this super voter, for 30-40 minutes, answer all their questions, walk away and feel like it was a great conversation. The exit survey would say, "Did you vote for John who spent 45 minutes talking with you about the subject?"

They answered, "No." "Why not?" "They didn't ask for my vote." I know. It sounds a little crazy.

You need to ask people to return to your school. You need to ask people to enroll. When we secret shop, no one asks. People just don't make the ask. They'll give you the enrollment package. They'll ask you if you have any questions. They'll sit patiently. They'll give you a great tour. The best ones will do all those things, and then they let you leave.

The funny thing is there's an old adage in car sales. I know. I'm talking about hamburgers. I'm talking about car sales. I'm talking about voters. It's all the science of human emotions and getting them to do something that you're asking. It's all the same science bucket. It's all the same cognitive basis. In car dealerships, they'll teach salespeople this technique all the time. I pretended to be a car salesman for a while and learn their training. I love watching great salespeople work because you can translate that knowledge. They would tell the salespeople, if they don't buy from you right now, they're going to buy. They're just not going to buy from you. They're going to leave the lot and buy wherever somebody makes a stronger ask. That's how you end up with pushy salespeople that are so scared that you're going to leave the lot. They know you're going to buy, but not from them.

You don't have to become a used car salesman. You don't have to become a salesman at all. I mean, all those jobs are awesome. I love car salesmen. I have a little bit of a car buying problem. I admit it. I need help. I'm not ready to go to rehab yet. You need to have a bit of this "make the ask, make people feel good" mentality. Principals, teachers, at the end of school, are you out in the parking lot at dropoff and pickup saying, "Thank you for being here. I want you back next year." You can't just say thank you for being here. You literally have to use the words, will you come back next year? That will help you with your retention rates.

It is hard to do. Who wants to go out there and sit in the sun? Who wants to go out there when it's raining and say those things? But you've got to do it. You've got to go out there and make that ask. You see these big buttons,

ENROLL NOW, on the websites. It's awesome. I hope I convinced you to make the ask. Now, I'm going to go secret shop at your school, and you're not going to do it, and I'm going to get frustrated. But I know it's hard.

The other thing that you've got to do is explain the why. You got to ask, and you've got to explain why. Why would I enroll? I'm going to give you one more thing on the ask. I just can't let it go, because I've been fighting with this for so many years. The number one reason why anyone gives to a nonprofit is because they are asked. It's not because they believe in the cause. It's not because they just wake up in the morning, and they feel like giving money to somebody. It's because somebody asked them to give, and then they give. So you have to ask.

Then you have to explain the why. I'm telling you, charter schools are the best at this. Homeschools are probably tied with public schools on describing the why, as in, why pick us. Then some private schools kind of fall next. It's kind of interesting. Some religious private schools don't make the ask as well, and they don't do the why, because mainly I think they have a reoccurring audience that's feeding their school population. You can discount that a bit. But public schools have to explain the why.

Why would they pick this particular school? Why would they pick this particular district? Once again, it's the competitive advantages. You should pick us, because we're the most geared toward making sure your children will be successful and ready for whatever they choose in life. That's a why. It's not very specific, but it's a why. In this advertisement for Freedom Prep, it says, "Why? It's because our mission is to prepare your students." Duh. What else would it be? But they still put it on their websites, and they still explain it.

I'm not going to get into every single reason why. You have to pick that. You should have figured out what makes your school or district unique and special, and you should still focus on safety. Safety can mean many different things. It can be bullying, gun violence, Covid–the source of fear can change, but the emotion remains. Your message should explain how you're going to keep parents' babies safe, how you're going to make their babies successful, and what competitive advantage your school has. Three things.

Now, let's get into some tactical stuff. We've been reviewing high-level messaging, high-level competitive advantage stuff. Now, let's get into some of the concrete tactics that your competition is using and that you can use to recruit and keep your students.

I don't expect you to do everything. I want you to do just slightly better. If you focus too much of your energy on just recruiting and retaining students through marketing and selling points and all these really tactical things I'm going to talk about, then I don't think you're spending enough time educating the children. I know that's your first mission. I know that's what you came to do. I know that's why you don't get paid enough because it's a passion job for you, and I want you to stay focused on that. I think that's the right thing to do. I just want you to do a little bit more over here to keep the students, so you can keep your budgets up.

Tactics: one, chatbots. The way chatbots work is they're on the website. They're programmed with hundreds of auto responses, but web visitors feel like they're talking to a real person. I don't know if this has ever happened to you. It's happened to me before, where you're on a website, and a little window pops up: "Hi, this is Maurice. Can I help you?" I want to reply to it, even though I know it's a computer, because I don't want to be rude. It's a bot. It's a computer program, and I have a hard time. It takes discipline to go, delete, delete, delete. Remember, your parents might think they're engaging with a real person. It's a good tool if you can add it to the website. We've done that for some districts.

Next, active social media. Competitors are often active on social media. They post frequently on the school or district's platforms. If you have a dedicated employee, and maybe it's not their full-time job, but it's a portion of their job, and they have a backup person, get crazy on social media. Make sure they have parameters, and they don't post things that could get you into trouble. But the main key with social media is you've got to keep up with it. This is the same issue with websites. Websites that have calendars that aren't kept up to date are worse than those that don't have them at all.

Related: marquees. You see those signs out in front of individual schools, and they say, "Christmas Break starts December 18th!" and it's like January 20th. It doesn't give you a lot of confidence if they can't keep their signs updated. It's better to get rid of that sign if you're not going to keep it updated. But how many teachers, principals, staff, went by those schools and didn't say anything about that marquee? How many people in charge of the marquee got upset that people were saying the marquee's out of date? They go, "I'm doing the best job I can do." No, you're not. Go pull it all down. Let me pull it down. That's hurting you because it makes it look like you're not detail oriented. It makes it look like you can't get the job done that you agreed to do.

That's what I mean. If you're going to do social media, don't turn it over to somebody for whom it's a hobby, and it just kind of works out if they post things whenever they post things. Don't turn it over to someone getting ready to retire in a year when you don't have a backup plan. It's better to just avoid social media if you can't maintain it because it makes you look like you can't focus on the details. Now, ideally, you have it, and it's active. When I mean active, reoccurring. It doesn't have to be daily. It doesn't have to be weekly, but it has to be enough activity that visitors think that you actually pay attention to it, and you post interesting things.

For websites and web calendars, if you're not going to put events on the calendar, just take the calendar feature off of your website. I know that there's some districts that have certain legal requirements to provide certain color fonts and items on their website. You have to keep it up to date, or you have to put a disclaimer that says, "We don't have the staff." I always love this disclaimer. "We are so busy teaching your children that you will find that this calendar will be out of date from time to time. Please let us know if you find an issue." What you're doing is you're advocating. You're saying where we're going to focus is on the babies, on training the children, not on some website.

Now before someone goes, "Brian said not to have these," yes, I want you to have calendars. I want you to have social media, too, if you can keep it up to date. I want you to have signs out in front of your schools if you can keep them up to date. If you can't, say uncle. Learn what to say no to and walk away. The hardest thing is saying no to good ideas, but that's what you have to do to be really competitive.

More and more tactics are out there. Testimonials—getting your parents to do a video or put a quote on a website—can be very effective. People love testimonials from real people. Not fake people, not paid people and not actors. They love testimonials. These charter schools are really capturing it. You've got fans out there. You've got parents who are supporters. Just get a quote. Stick it on your website. Put it on a flyer. I love this. If you can get parents to give the tours of your school, or even students, A-plus.

A lot of you do tours, and so does your competition. Elsewhere in the book, you'll see a whole section on giving VIP tours. These can be critical.

Another tactic: earned media. Now, earned media is a term in the communications world, which means free. You have paid media, and you have earned. Earned media can tell great stories. Now, I will say this. A lot of the so-called "earned media," like opinion pieces you read in newspapers, letters to the editor or articles written by the paper about a subject, are paid. It may also be there is something in the story that lets the people that are writing it have motivation to write it. Now, it could just be you keep pitching stories to news sources, and we love that. Keep pitching ideas to your local media.

At good, sound local media outlets, it's not a pay-to-play scheme, but articles like this can be bought. There are all kinds of services you can pay to get articles printed, and you see this a lot with list articles. I was trying to find a new leaf blower, and what do you Google? Top 10 blowers. When a parent is Googling top schools in their area, they'll see these articles pop up, and a lot of them are paid to have been written or paid to have been placed as a higher search result. Some of them are just good old fashioned articles covered by real media sources. You need to cultivate that. You need to start developing relationships with reporters and local radio shows. This is a capacity issue. You have to have the resources to do it, but it's very cool because people will read this stuff and think you're the cat's meow, and that gets them really interested in your school.

Once again, more tactics. Remember, this is what the competition is doing right now to get your students, and if you've got the resources and the time, you need to think about doing some of this. It's just good old fashioned grassroots organizing. We learned a lot about grassroots organizing through running census campaigns for the United States government through one of our sister companies, and getting parents to fill out census data is really tough. With grassroots efforts, you're going door-to-door, finding out who's moved to the area and potentially finding new parents. Or you may be finding out what parents go to your school and which ones are the most at risk of leaving. Your competition will figure out your most vulnerable targets, and they will actively try to recruit them. They will go to the door. They will show up at community events in the neighborhood, they'll explain why, and they'll make the ask.

On top of that, your competition is making phone calls–phone banking. One of the things that we have learned through recruiting students back is door knocking and face-to-face is invaluable, but it's really expensive. It's really time consuming. Phone banking is relatively expensive, but it can go a lot faster. We utilize a lot of phone banking, making tens of thousands of calls in a week. There are a lot of protocols for great customer service that happen in those phone calls. But generally, competitors who phone bank are calling your families, making the ask and offering the why.

Another strategy: giveaways. You don't have anything to give away. Your budgets are tight enough. You don't have permission. You can't bribe them. Does it feel like a bribe? It feels like a bribe. If it walks like a duck and talks like a duck, it's probably a duck. Some of your competition are giving away vacations, giving away free iPads, giving away computers, giving away gas cards. You can't compete with that. If that's what they want, you have to keep selling what makes you awesome because you're not going to give them free stuff.

Certainly, they're doing mass text messages and emails. Email is a great form of communication, mainly because it's so cheap, and people keep their email address longer now than they keep a home. Think about that. It used to be that you'd keep a home for seven or eight years. Now you keep an email address for 20. I know guys who still have AOL accounts. I didn't know AOL was still a thing, but they have AOL accounts.

We talked earlier about this targeting going on. They are figuring out who your parents are, and they are going after them. These are the same tactics that we use to recruit and keep students when we work with districts. I need you to understand, they're very data driven. We talk about the art and science of communication or of running a great campaign to recruit or keep a student. The messaging is all the art. Your competitive advantage? That's all the art. The science is this tracking and all these different tactical things that they do. Door knocks, phone calls, emails. You're going to see them in neighborhoods with clipboards and shirts and signs. We believe that it's best to go toe-to-toe with that kind of activity, but this is the new landscape.

I'm going to get into one last subject. I want to expose you to just how many resources your competition is putting to bear on getting your students. Once again, I am not asking for perfection. I don't think you should spend as much as they spend on marketing and communication. You need to spend some, and you need to be really tactical about it. You need to really use art and science in order to get those students, but the percentages of their overall budget that these charter and private schools are using just for marketing and recruitment efforts is shocking.

The final image in the art spread below shows that in this particular district, its second line item, its second most expensive line item, is student recruiting at nearly $300,000. They spend $1.2 million for teachers and administrative staff and all the people to actually train the babies. They have a management fee listed at $271,000. Payroll and taxes. This is the way to look at it. Instructional supplies and textbooks are $241,000, but student recruitment is $291,000. They're spending more money to recruit than they are on textbooks and supplies. I'm going to say it again. *They are spending more money to recruit students than they are on textbooks and supplies.* What? That's how serious they are about taking your students. Remember, when your student leaves, so does their funding.

The funny thing is the district separates marketing. Marketing is another $56,000. That means almost $350,000 of a budget that's got to be around $2 million is devoted to these tactics to get students from public schools. Around $2 million, and they're spending $350,000 just to go get your students. That's a big percentage. Don't do that, but get in the game. The charter schools are smaller and have smaller budgets, and they always spend more than the public schools. That's a massive takeaway with which I want you to leave.

I want you to understand you're awesome. You've got innovative, exciting things about your school, your classroom. If you're in charge of the grounds of a school, the maintenance department, there are wonderful things going on there, and I want you to start thinking about what makes you special. What's your competitive advantage? I want you to start explaining it to people. I want you to say why you're special. That's by individual school or individual district. I want you to structure the why parents should choose your school because that's what your competition is doing. They're out there competing against you, and you need to compete, too. It's America, and that's fair. It's cool.

All too often, public school staff and faculty are absorbed by the curriculum. They want to train the babies, and they don't want to have to sell. They don't want to market, but we need you. We need you to market, or your school population is going to dwindle because your competition is marketing whether you do it or not.

Once you've got your why, I need you to ask people to enroll. I need you to ask people to come back. I need you to thank them. I need you to use those specific words because they need to hear it. Then I want you to start thinking about the tactical issues that you're covering already, what you're doing really well, and what you just don't have the time and the resources to do. I'd rather you do fewer things pretty good than do a bunch of things poorly. Don't have a vigorous social media account and all these different platforms, Tik Tok and LinkedIn and Instagram and Facebook, if you can't maintain them all. It would be better just to have one. I know somebody said, "We need them." If they're done poorly, you don't. Poorly makes you look poor. You want to look awesome, and so I want you to focus on those things that you can handle exceptionally well.

Make that ask. Give them that why. Understand the different tactical things you could pick, too. Maybe you could pick up one tactical idea you heard, take it back to your school district, and start to implement it. Best of luck beating the competition.

Delivering High-Quality Education, No Matter the Zip Code

Charter schools are built on the belief that kids come first. They keep red tape and bureaucracy out of public education and give passionate teachers the freedom to do what they do best: teach. That means that charter schools are launching bright futures and sending more kids to college, especially in communities where high-quality schools are needed most.

The implication of this ad is pretty clear: they care about all the children. This implies you don't. We all know this is bunk because the law actually requires us to teach ALL children while our competition is not bound by the same rules.

Notice the charter school is making the argument that they focus on success, which is different from the competition. We all know this isn't true, but it is a clever marketing strategy.

In these two examples, the schools have a competitive advantage: flexibility. The schools are attempting to sell the flexible nature of online schools. And while in person public schools cannot offer this degree of flexibility, it doesn't mean that is what parents want. This is just one simple thing that they chose to highlight because they are lacking many of your competitive advantages. They are simply highlighting one thing they believe they do better.

This is a classic attack ad. I'm sure you all have seen so many of these in political candidate races that they almost seem like standard marketing practices. And while it is true that negative ads work (sorry they do, that's why they have been around for hundreds of years), it's a real shame these types of ads are now being used to get a parent to pick a new school.

This is a classic example of using an analogy to create a positive message that will in turn create a connection between their school and being smart, like a great chess player.

5

Behind the Scenes

reasons
why you should
homeschool

BeautyofSelah.com

Your competition is using the power of clickbait to begin to sell their narratives. Take this example of a seemingly helpful story to give parents an unbiased view of the benefits of homeschool. It doesn't look like a typical ad, but is certainly designed to get parents to buy homeschool. This is especially true as you read the five reasons (see below).

2. I want them to keep their innocence.

When we were stationed in Hawaii I was a part of a large wives page on Facebook. On the page, spouses would ask questions relating to living there, the army, and food among many other things.

I will never ever forget a post from a mom who just moved there and posted about how her kindergartner got an entire lesson on sex on the bus ride home. And then other mother's commented saying "that's just how it is here, the bus driver doesn't pay attention" "my kid learned about it at recess" "teach them at home if you don't want them to know".

My jaw dropped.

I shouldn't have to be on defense of what my children will be exposed to at such an early age. I had my innocence ripped from me as a child, I refuse to allow that to happen to my children. Does that mean that I want to shelter them?

This is the second "secret" to consider homeschool. Notice the overt tug and your heart to protect and keep children safe. When the truth is everyone eventually loses their innocence, the only question I have for this school is will you prepare your children for success in the real world?

One thing we can all do better is explain "WHY" the families should choose us. This is simple and needs to be done on all marketing materials including our websites.

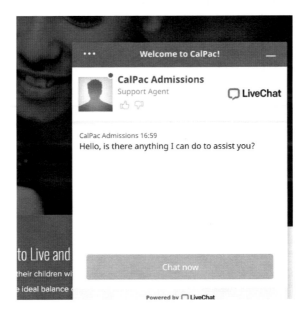

While we don't have the resources to use every piece of technology that exists, it is helpful to understand that much of our competition is using the same marketing strategies as large corporations.

The KIPP Difference, According to Parents

Sheree Graham
Parent, KIPP Nashville

Testimonials are powerful tools to recruit families.

charter school innovation

Victoria Harker January 19, 2021 4 min read Add comment

A new national report card places Arizona as the top state in the nation for a friendly regulatory environment that encourages charter schools to grow and excel. As a result, Arizona has one of the most robust and diverse charter school systems in the country, according to the report.

For families, that equates into more options to find a school that fits their children's unique needs, said Jake Logan, president and CEO of the nonprofit Arizona Charter Schools Association.

"This indicates what we already know in Arizona, that we have a really great environment for innovation and for charter schools to flourish," Logan said. "There's always tweaks and needed changes and reforms that we can and should discuss, but overall we have a really healthy charter school sector and I think they are serving students very well."

Arizona ranked number one for its charter school laws in the 2020 report from the nonprofit Center for Education Reform in Washington, D.C., which advocates for school choice.

Jake Logan

It was the only state to receive an "A" grade in the report. The study researched and assessed charter school laws in all states, analyzing the impact of state law on charter schools, the robustness of the charter sector, the diversity of schools and charter school policy and regulation.

Atmosphere that encourages innovation and teacher freedom

Earned media is simply the use of writing and getting placed stories in local papers, blogs, etc. But times have changed, and while many of these articles look and feel like unbiased reporters are writing them, many are actually paid placement.

Your competition uses live calling, canvas operations and other grassroots marketing techniques to get their messages out. But don't worry, we do too.

Freedom Preparatory Academy
August 26, 2020 ·

Kindergarten parent? Looking for a great school? Look no further than Freedom Prep! Free iPad, small classes, and internet support provided for 2020-21.

Message us today to start your child's journey to college!

💙👍😮 176   26 Comments 17 Shares

👍 Like   💬 Comment   ↪ Share

One way we are truly at a disadvantage is that we cannot induce families to join us with gifts.

Success Academy Williamsburg, Top Five Expenditures, 2011-2013

Budget Item	Expenditure
Salaries	$1,189,598.00
Student Recruitment	$291,187.00
Management Fee	$271,012.00
Payroll Taxes and Employee Benefits	$258,821.00
Instructional Supplies and Textbooks	$241,301.00
Teacher Recruitment	$49,767.00
Marketing	$56,908.00

The charter school above invests nearly $300,000 in student recruitment expenses, and this doesn't include their marketing budget of $56,000. These combined expenses total more than the school invests in instructional supplies and textbooks.

SECTION VI:

REPUTATION BUILDING

Throughout this book, I'm really trying to offer the tactics or the rules that will really help you in the day-to-day activities I believe are necessary to recruit and keep more students. It's really at the ground level, so to speak. For the next series of rules, I want to step back and give you more of a 20,000-foot overview on what the individual schools and districts need to do to build long-lasting stable reputations community members view with reverence. I want people to think, that's a *great* school, not a good school. Even if it's not factually true. I think that that happens all too often. For some reason, schools can get reputations, just like people can. The next series of rules are going to lay out in quick order, almost in a rapid-fire session, some of the fundamental things that I think you should be thinking about in the long-term.

Now, this is not an in-depth course on reputation building. That's a book for another day, but here are some of the rules that will have the greatest impact on your district.

RULE 1

PRIORITY IS NOT PLURAL

It's really funny that you'll be in different organizations, and they'll say things like, "We have eight moon missions." I guess the moon is the preferred analogy because it's both distant and visible, like so many goals. You can see it, but the work to get there is great. Then somebody will say, "But we only have one moon." It's a joke but a powerful statement, which is that the word priority is not plural. Priority means number one. In our society we have such a hard time saying no to things that we will try to have multiple priorities. The truth is that those priorities will collide at some point, either because you have a lack of time, a lack of resources like money or people to implement those priorities, or because they actually just become completely in conflict with one another.

Let me give you one example of how priorities can conflict. Some humans say, "I want everyone to love me, and I want to be a person that gets things done." That sounds really good in theory, but in practicality, at some point there's going to be a conflict between those two reputation standards. If you want everybody to like you, then you can't force activities or deadlines because sometimes forcing people to complete tasks makes them not like you very much. The reputations to be liked by a team and to accomplish many goals as a team will come into conflict. You must choose one. If you don't know what your priority is—what one main thing that you want everyone to know about you or your school or your district—then you're going to get off track.

It is unbelievably difficult to sit down and decide on a reputation priority. There can only be one *most important* aspect of your reputation you want people to know. You've really got to sweat this out. But you must choose one. Diluting your reputation by asking people to remember too many things about your district has serious consequences: your district will be known for nothing.

You can be known for one thing globally and even regionally. Everything else must be a later addition once they've gotten to know you. To start, you have to fixate.

I would suggest the priority is we are focused on our children. That seems simple, but if that is your priority every single day, you will do everything right. Everything behind that priority will fix itself. If taking care of the babies, the children, is the main thing, then you'll know how to deal with bullies. You'll know how to deal with a violent situation. You'll know what academic tests are right and wrong.

I understand that a lot of these things are not within your control, but the point is that you cannot have multiple priorities, so stop it. Pick one thing and drive that until you accomplish it.

RULE 2

GET BORED WITH YOUR MESSAGE

There's an old axiom in political conversations that once you're bored with your message, they've just started to listen. Let's assume that you've decided your priority is you want people to think you're the most academically rigorous middle school in the area. You want to be known for your academics. So all of your messaging (and messaging is followed up in later rules) is related to that one central priority, that one central theme that our school is the best at educating children.

You're going to develop a speech. You're going to develop some talking points. You're going to have some literature, maybe some signs on your walls. You're going to come in and out of that school, day in and day after, and after some period of time, you're going to be really sick of seeing it. You're going to say, "Now is the time to redo it." I'm begging you, do not do that. When you're sick of looking at it, the people have just started to pay attention to it.

You've got to get unbelievably bored with what you're putting out to the world because people are busy. People have many, many other things going on, which means it takes them significantly longer to even first notice the message you've crafted. And because they're just noticing the message, it will have no impact if you change it. If you keep changing the needle about what you want to be known for, you're never going to have the impact you want. I'm begging you. Get bored with your message, and then when somebody says, "We need to freshen this up," say, "As long as it stays to our priority, as long as it stays to the same theme, we can adjust the words a little bit, but we cannot change course." We have to spend years building our reputation, not weeks.

RULE 3
KEEP IT SHORT AND SIMPLE

The first time I heard about the KISS philosophy it was in the military, where they refer to it's full meaning as "Keep it simple, stupid." I like keep it short and simple instead, but I know there are a lot of iterations on what this means. Essentially, the expression means if you want to be known for something, and you're trying to get a message out to the community about who you are, it's got to be short. It's got to be brief.

Crafting strong content is further discussed in the rule Developing 3-2-1 Messaging, but this short and simple KISS rule is also important and deserves its own space. You're going to sit with lawyers and board members and faculty and parents, and everyone cares, and everyone wants your organization to do great, and they're so excited. They want to sell, sell, sell what you're doing great in the community. Your job as the leader is to say, "We got to keep it simple. We got to keep it brief. We got to get bored with our message, and we can have one priority."

All these rules for building a great reputation are you've got to get to be known for one thing, and the only way to really do that is to get bored, to keep it simple, really brief, follow that 3-2-1 message system, and then we fall into our next rule.

RULE 4

SELL YOURSELF, NO ONE ELSE WILL

I have an entire book on media training in which I reference some of the rules in this book. One of the main missteps that public schools too often make is they forget to sell themselves. They forget to actually convey how awesome and great they are. For hundreds of years, they didn't have to sell themselves. Public school was there, and it was awesome, and that's where we got to train the next generation, and that's what helped keep our culture alive. They weren't in the selling business.

Now, with the advent of all this competition, from charter schools to homeschools to private schools, if you don't start to sell–if you don't start to bang on your drum a little bit and explain to people why you're awesome sauce–then no one else is going to do that for you. Your competition is selling themselves.

Know this, I have traveled around the country, training and visiting schools for a decade. We only represent traditional public schools because they're the best. They're the ones that even with limited resources, even being outgunned, so to speak, by their competition, provide a better education for the children, in my opinion. I want you to get excited, and I want you to start putting out those positive messages that still fit your one priority. Keep it simple but keep pounding. Keep selling whatever you're doing that's awesome.

A few examples have broken my heart over the years, where public schools didn't think they had anything to sell. In one case, it was a very big district, 90,000+ students. I went to meet with them, and the communications director was there and the superintendent and the chief of staff. Somebody spoke up, and they said, "We don't have anything to sell, Brian." It crushed my soul. They were so beaten down. At this point in time, legislation was pulling resources from them, giving it to other schools. The papers were beating up on them because there were new shiny objects out there. Reporters love to write on new schools and shiny buildings. They were a little beaten down.

We had to sit down and uncork that a little bit to show them how many things they were doing great. They were in the fishbowl, so to speak, and they didn't realize how great they were. They weren't selling themselves because they were frozen with being berated for too long.

I want you to get excited. I want you to feel awesome about who you are. This school had so many great things. They had faculty who'd won Teacher of the Year awards. They had kids from poor, at-risk communities getting unbelievable scholarships to some of the top schools in the nation. They had really unique specialty programs. They had clerical workers running clubs because they wanted to help the children. They were doing so many cool things, and once we freed that up they started having the ability to sell themselves.

In another situation, there was a district with maybe 2,000 students. It was a very small district, a very rural area of the country. No major city nearby. Homeschools and one private school were the main competitors. I really liked the superintendent. He was a young guy with a great staff, and he was having some problems. They said, "We can't compete with the competition."

I understood what he was saying. The private school in the area had additional resources and a newer building. Then I saw it: drones running over a football field. There were lines of children learning how to use them. I asked about the drones, and he replied, "That's a program that we put together because there are huge Amazon warehouses in the area." The median household income in the community was $25,000 or $28,000, and because of this program, a person could potentially graduate from high school with a certificate in flying a drone, work at these warehouses and make $60,000 to $70,000.

I said, "How many children are you limited to do that for?" They go, "No, no. We got a grant from some people, and we invested. Any child can take it." I said, "You're not selling that?" That is one of the most awesome programs about which I've ever heard, and that's a competitive advantage, and it shows that you're innovative, you're technologically sound, and you're preparing the children for the future. He couldn't see it because he was in the fishbowl. He didn't know how great the school was.

I want you to feel comfortable selling who you are and putting out information that lets you know how great you are. I'll give you one more example. We take a lot of tours, and we secret shop at a lot of schools around the nation to get a sense of the landscape. We don't just shop public schools, but all types of schools. We even visit colleges, for that matter, because I like to see how they give tours, so we can learn how public schools can improve their own. During the tours, it's funny how many people point out the problems I didn't even notice. "Try to ignore the carpet. It hasn't been replaced in years. Ignore the spider webs in the corner." I didn't even notice the spiders. I didn't even notice the carpet. I was too busy looking at the awesome artwork up and down the hallway. People are focusing on negatives too much and not positives.

Along with the Developing 3-2-1 Messaging rule, which is the last rule in this series, these reputation rules are all about selling yourself. You've got to keep it short. Get bored with your messaging, and really stick to your guns on having one top thing that you want to be known for, and you're going to start building a better reputation, which in turn is going to help you recruit and keep more of your students.

RULE 5
DEVELOP 3-2-1 MESSAGE POINTS

During this next rule, we are going to work on developing powerful messaging: soundbites. The reason why this is so vital is because the world's a busy place. I want you to have clear, concise ways to communicate with your target audience. Your target audience is the group of people with whom you're trying to communicate. If you're a teacher, is it parents during a conference? If you're the principal, is it the faculty, staff or the community at large? You must decide on your target audience and tailor your message to that group. Then you must make sure your message is concise enough to have an impact.

Building powerful messaging starts with research on a tactic called 3-2-1 messaging. In short, the research has proven repeatedly that people can typically remember up to three main pieces of information. Any more than this number tends to be forgotten. Some people can remember four or five things. Some people can only remember two, but on average the bulk of humans out there can remember three big data points.

Your social security number is broken down into three blocks. The reason for the dashes is to divide it up into three little blocks, so you can retain the information. Your phone number, by the way, is in three blocks: area code, first three digits, then four. I know, somebody's going to say, "Not if you're calling internationally." You don't know your international code. You look it up, because you're not remembering it. Don't be a smart aleck. You get my point here. If you're questioning the three blocks of information, do your own research. It's out there. It exists.

So we're going to always have up to three message points—not four, not five and never 10,000. We're going to have up to three. Having one or two message points is even better because fewer are easier to digest.

Let's discuss the 2-1. Each one of those *three* message points should be *up to* 21 words. Yes, you have to actually count them. Twenty-one words for Message Point 1. Twenty-one words for Message Point 2. Twenty-one words for Message Point 3. This equates to the length of time it takes to do an elevator speech. It's about 14 seconds. Now, if you're from the South like me, it's about 21 words. You could probably get a few more words in if you talk more quickly, but this is a good number to gauge. When you first write your message points, I know it's going to be more. It's never fewer, for some reason. "I got 38 words, Brian. It's perfect." No, it's not. Edit it. Edit it. Edit it. Make it more concise. Brevity is a virtue.

I'm going to explain to you why brevity is such a virtue. The world is overwhelming with content right now. Everything's just becoming background noise because there are so many billboards, video ads, static ads, and TV, radio and podcast commercials. Messaging is overwhelming. Emails arrive. Text messages notify us all day. If you want to impact your audience, if you actually want people to listen to you, you've got to cut through all that noise.

My question for you is how many messages do we get in a day? In the United States, dusk to dawn, when you're up, you're paying attention. Harvard did a study years ago, and it said you're getting as many as 10,000 messages per day. This study is old. Some people say it's now as many as 15,000. Fifteen thousand messages a day. How is your message going to get through to your target audience?

The crux of all this is–take me at my word–people don't care what you want to convey. People do not care about your message, no matter how important it is, no matter how awesome it is. OK, maybe some people care. But you have to take the stance that people are busy. They're trying to pay their bills. They're trying to do their own jobs. They're trying to get their own points across to the rest of the world, and they can't consume 10,000 or 15,000 messages a day. So they pick and choose. The most impactful messages are going to be the ones that are going to penetrate through the noise by getting their attention.

I know a lot of us grew up with this idea that you've got to be an active listener. It is your job to pay attention. Well, that's true to a degree. If you're in a classroom setting, and you're going to get graded, it's absolutely your responsibility to pay attention. If you're an employee, and you're getting paid, it's absolutely your responsibility. But the general world is busy, and even in employment situations, everyone has 25 things to do. Which one are they going to do? The one that they understand the most. The one that's the clearest, and the one that's the simplest. The other ones suffer from vaguery. Ambiguity leads to inaction.

If you're counting on your audience to be active listeners, you're failing on the front end. Yes, we want them to be active listeners. Yes, I would love to train you to be an active listener in your own life, but right now we're talking about you as the conveyor of information, and it's your responsibility, no one else's, to pay attention.

Years ago, I was prepping a client. They were going to meet with the governor of a particular state, and they had a laundry list of funding initiatives to request. I'm sitting down, and we're working with the superintendent and a couple board members who are going to meet with the governor. I said, let's get your messaging clear. I'm happy to help. They had 27 points they wanted to cover. Twenty-seven distinct things that they wanted to convey to the governor. I was like, "How long are you going to be with the governor?" They reply, "Fifteen minutes–give or take." I said, "Well, I think you ought to take this book and throw it out the window." Of course, they responded, "What do you mean, Brian? We've got to get this through to the governor. He has to understand." I said, "No, no, no. He does not have to understand anything. You want him to understand things. You're asking him to understand things, but he is his own independent individual, and he has to do whatever is right for his life. You want him, that's different. If you want him to understand something, you better use brevity as a virtue. You better simplify it. With 15 minutes, I'm not even going to ask you to do three message points. I'm going to ask you to do one or none."

I know. They said, "None?" I was like, "You could have more impact on the governor if you walked in and said, 'I got a laundry list of things to do. I got 27 things. You can't consume that in a 15-minute long meeting. Your time is valuable. Let me ask you what I can do for you, and maybe at some point we can have a longer meeting, and we can really dig into these facts. Maybe I can meet with a staffer and get this summarized in a way that could have an impact on you.'"

That's one message point. I said none, but it's really one: "What can I do for you?" That's a really powerful message point. They didn't want to do that, of course. So I said, "We got to simplify this down to one primary thing. What's your one primary ask? We've got to really get that message point. If he has questions, you can follow it up with all these extra data points." But when you try to overwhelm people, they get nothing. It just becomes white noise. This has happened to you. You know you've sat in meetings, you've sat in presentations, where information just washed over you. I want you to remember that when you're speaking.

I've got a concept I always talk about called speaker's amnesia. When you're sitting as an audience member, you notice everything that the person's doing wrong. You say things such as, "That's a terrible eulogy," or "Oh, my God, that YouTube video's bad" and "That commercial, I don't even know what they were selling in it." But then when you get in charge, for some reason you start to think that everyone is paying attention. That's really what I want to get across to you right now. You have to assume they're busy, so consolidate your message points.

They did, and they met with the governor. They took one key message point. They actually stayed because they had one key message point, and the governor gave them about 25 minutes because he was very curious about those topics. They set a follow up meeting, and they started to get slowly into the other points over time. They started to digest my advice. He was going to get all those 27 points eventually, but they rushed it, they're going to get nothing at all across. The complexity was worth a two-hour conversation, and with time, they ended up getting a lot further than they'd even hoped because they'd really consolidated.

> **TIP: Just take that in mind and realize that people are busy. Somebody's mad at me right now. "Brian, you said people don't care about what I'm saying." I'm just saying they're busy, and they're overwhelmed. They will care if you can cut through the noise. The gist is you've got to have brevity. It's a virtue, and you've got to cut all this stuff down.**

Let's get into developing your message. Soundbites, elevator speeches and powerful messaging are the same thing. I may bounce around a little bit. I want you to start with deciding to whom you are trying to communicate? You've got to consider, how do they need to consume the information? What do they need to hear to have impact? I'm not asking you to change your goals. I'm not asking you to change your mission, but you've got to word it in slightly different ways.

Let's assume that you are a principal or communications officer at a school district, and you've got to convey the same message to lots of different people. Maybe it's the closing of a school–a very touchy subject. What you're conveying to board members and to your teammates, your employees, the staff, the parents, and even the schoolchildren, is going to be different for each group, even though it's consistently about the closing of a school. You talk to third graders differently from the way you talk to board members and differently from how you'd explain to parents.

Board members, if they're elected, are going to worry about the outcry. They're going to worry about overall budget concerns, the overall mission. What I've found is if they don't have the messaging on the reason why this school has to be shut down, they'll be confronted by parents at a grocery store. Your board members will be at a grocery store, and they'll get yelled at by the public. They need to have their one or two quick soundbites to explain why, so that they can protect and advocate for the position of the school district. You would actually give them the talking points to convey to others. That's a different message. One of the messages would be, we're going to give you exactly what you need to advocate for this issue. That's your first message point. Then the next two may be exactly what they're advocating.

But to parents, you're directly advocating. To staff members, your most important message will be, "We're closing a school, but we're not making cuts. You're not going to lose your job." The parents don't have to hear that they're not losing their jobs, but the staff members better know that they're safe, or you're going to have your good ones take off. If you want to keep your best and brightest, which I know you do, you better have a message that compels them to stay. So you see how even a simple message must be tailored to different audiences.

Now, someone might say, "We need a message for the media–the reporters. We need to develop talking points for them." No, you don't. They're not your audience. They are a vehicle to communicate to your audience. They're important, but they are a platform. If you run a TV commercial, if you talk to a reporter, if you run an internet ad, if you send an email, these are all platforms. An email is a vehicle to communicate with a target audience. A video is a vehicle to talk to a target audience. The media is a vehicle to talk to a target audience. Worry about the target audience, not the vehicle. In this case, it could be parents. It could be alumni. List all those potential target audiences. Develop a couple core message points, and then see if they work for each group. If they don't, then adjust.

TIP: Focus on the target audience first. Figure out your target audiences across the board. Then, once you've got messages developed for each target, then start considering how to use emotions–pathos–to make an impact. When you're developing message points, if they're too data heavy or too factual in nature, you're not reaching most of your audience. Write your talking points, and then consider if you've considered emotions or based them primarily on facts and data.

I'm going to use the character Commander Spock from *Star Trek*. Fictional Spock was from planet Vulcan, known throughout the universe for its inhabitants' logical, cold dispositions. They rarely showed emotion. Imagine Spock was going to go buy a car and had two cars on a lot, the Cadillac Escalade and a minivan. The Escalade was more expensive than the minivan but had the same crash test rating. Same gas mileage. Seats all leather. It can fit the same number of people. Which one would Spock pick? Spock, being purely logical, is going to pick the minivan over and over again. He doesn't care about his image. He doesn't care about how it makes him feel when he drives it. It's a utilitarian vehicle, and he wants to go from A to F. That's all he cares about.

There are many people who will pick the minivan, but if they had unlimited money, would they still pick the minivan? I love driving a minivan. When I go and rent a car for live trainings, I rent a minivan, and it's awesome. I can fit my bike gear in it. I'm in a captain's seat. But emotionally, I can't *buy* a minivan. It's ridiculous. I know it's ego driven. I still don't want the minivan as a permanent car even though I'd love it. If I had a backup minivan, I'd end up driving it all the time. I could say, "I'm driving a minivan today, but I've got a Cadillac Escalade–something big and manly!" But emotionally, it's hard. There's science that argues most of us are emotionally driven. Just around 20 percent of us are always going to be logical. Engineers can be like this. They might drive the minivan based purely on the deduction that it's illogical not to do so. They're right. I–much like more of the population–just emotionally can't handle that.

People make decisions based on their emotions, and then they typically use facts to justify their emotional decisions. When you're developing your talking points, you need to leverage emotion. You figured out your targets. Take parents, for instance. They're afraid. They're nervous. As a parent I understand this. I want my child to grow up, get out of the house and get a job. I want her to be safe when she goes to school. All of these ideas are very emotional. There's no reason for me to think she's not going to be safe. But I see TV news and headlines and get nervous. Emotion drives me to have concern about safety, and I decide it's a priority–then, only after deciding, do I use facts to justify its importance.

Another useful tip for developing lasting messages is to use figurative language. Metaphors, and analogies paint visuals in the mind. Consider this one, "It's like trying to fill the bathtub with the drain open." Here's another example in which an astronaut was trying to convey the danger of space flight. He said, "Any one flight in space on the space shuttle is as dangerous as 60 combat missions during wartime." The astronaut is trying to draw a comparison in terms of what people might be more likely to know and understand.

People typically understand wartime combat missions more than they understand space shuttles, but he could have picked an analogy that was even closer to them. "It's like playing Russian roulette with a revolver with two bullets in the chamber." That's a very real analogy people can imagine. The combat mission may have been a little too distant. It's kind of like saying how far is the moon from the Earth? It's 387,000 miles. Nobody can digest miles. Nobody can digest seconds and minutes. You've got to make an analogy.

Another tool for messaging is wit. A witty message I've used before is, "Are you going to let perfect be the enemy of better?" A lot of times, you'll be trying to launch a project, or you'll be trying to get people on board with a new curriculum or trying to get a new playground built. Let's take the playground example. You have some federal money. You have some state money. People submit designs for this playground. All too often, you'll get a large group of people who say, "I want these 10 things in this playground," and it is perfect. You can only get seven of them because of budgetary needs. They are against it because it's not perfect. "Why are we even building it, if it's not perfect? If it's not perfect, I do not want it." Wait a minute. We have a playground with two things in it right now, and they're broken. We can get something with seven that work, but you're against it because it's not perfect? You're going to let perfect be the enemy of better. So in the playground messaging, we have a desperate need to provide a safe playground for our children. That's point one. The secondary point is that anything is better than what we have now. The witty point might not necessarily be the main driver point, the main mission, but you can see how it's powerful enough to make an impact on the audience.

Rhetorical questions and folksy expressions can be effective. Take this one for example: "How many times are we going to gamble with lives, economies, and ecosystems?" It's rhetorical because of course no one wants to gamble with any of those things. Folksy is good, if you can get away with it, and if it makes sense for the target audience. This is one quote: "When you hear somebody say, this is not about money, it's about money. When you hear somebody say, this is not about sex, it's about sex." Now, that's pretty powerful. If you hear somebody say, "This is not about me," I know it's about you, and I know that you are trying to disarm me by saying it's not about you, but it is about you, and you believe it's about you. Those are kind of cute, but a little too folksy can be dangerous. Be a little careful there.

The first time you're going to write, you're going to use the actual data. It's normal. It's logical. Let's take the shutting down of a school as an example. We are going to save $3.2 million annually by shutting this school down. Well, that's true. It's accurate. It's factual, but don't use numbers. Write down the number the first time, but now you need to find an analogy on how that $3.2 million will connect with your target audience.

For example, by shutting down this school, we will save every other high school sports program across the entire school district, which equals about $3.2 million annually. Now, once again, I'm guessing on what $3.2 million equals and how much all these sports programs are. Go look in the budget and find things that will connect with them. Maybe the $3.2 million annually allows us to buy new computers for everyone in the school. Maybe $3.2 million annually allows us to have food programs for those most in need. These are analogies with which people can connect and that they can visualize. You notice they're emotional, right? The data, the number, is buying the minivan. The analogy is getting to people to understand, lean into their emotional quotient on this one. You can say $3.2 million, but make it real by finding things that you will get to keep because you've cut that school out.

Social statistics are relatively unfeeling. You can use statistics to prove a lot of great points, but, once again, they're not very emotionally grounded, unless the statistic has some sort of emotional component. In your talking points, I don't like a lot of statistics. I like statistics in the supporting documentation. I want you to have all the supporting documents. I want you to have reams of things that support the three talking points. I want you to answer all the people's questions when they start discussing the talking points. I want all that data. If you give a board member their talking points, you better have the supporting documents to back them up. What are the reasons why we need a new school? We need you to prove these bonds. Not for us, but for the future of our community. Future of our community? That begs a question. I love a talking point that begs a question because now you're having a dialogue. When people are having a dialogue, they're going to learn exactly what you want to convey to them, if you have all your homework done. Message points can open up a dialogue.

You don't want to open up a dialogue if the talking point is on a TV commercial. That's not the place you put the open-ended question or try to create a dialogue. Social media could be a space for dialogue if you've got somebody to respond. Just keep thinking about that target audience and the vehicle that you're using to get the information out. These things will start to work themselves out, but be strategic now anyway. Be thinking about the different ways these messages are going to be conveyed. Then edit them and write. Go and use a red pen.

There are great soundbites I think we all remember. A popular one is Franklin Roosevelt: "The only thing we have to fear is fear itself." Here's another soundbite: "Cleaning a house with a toddler in it is a lot like brushing your teeth while eating Oreos." I don't know what they were trying to pitch, but it certainly is funny, and it's certainly powerful, and I remember it. This last one is, "Money doesn't grow on trees, but it does grow faster in credit unions without those greedy bank fees." That lets you know that this message is supporting a credit union, and it's already conveying that bank fees are greedy. Bankers are greedy. Wow. They're leaning into kind of a stereotype. Sorry. It's a powerful message.

Remember, you don't have to reinvent the wheel. You can sponge other creative ideas that other school districts, other individual schools and classrooms, have utilized. I always like these: "rated a top school in the nation," "best high school for math," or "most challenging," and "reinventing education." That last one is only two words, but it sparks creativity. It sparks the question, what do you mean reinventing?

Of the three message points for any school or any school district, you've got to have two that relate to what we know from national polling data, which is that parents and caregivers want to know, will my child be safe? Safety can mean different things from gun violence to bullying to Covid. In the book section titled The Competition, we talk about how charter schools, private schools and homeschools, are recruiting your students, and they will use safety as a big issue. They will imply that public schools are not safe compared to their education model. If you're talking to a parent, if you feel like they don't think their children are safe, you better have a talking point about your safety protocols. You better have a talking point about why children at your school or district are going to be in a safe environment.

According to our national poll, one of your three talking points should be about making students successful. Success means different things to different people. To some it may mean college or a trade or simply moving out of the house. Whatever the case, you want to press that your school will make its students successful.

The third message point should be something very particular to your individual school. I do know what the order should be. You should lead with your second most powerful talking point. Some people will say it's your most powerful. Keep in mind that people tend to remember your last talking point. If you're only going to get one out, go with your most powerful one. If your strength is safety, talk about safety. If your strength, your competitive advantage, is success, talk about that.

TIP: The one thing that we started with today in this course was 3-2-1, simplicity. Brevity is a virtue. Keep It Simple. I don't want you to dumb down the information, but you do need to write it in a ninth-grade level. I don't want you to try to sound smart. If you're trying to sound smart, you're off your mission goal. If your mission goal is to sound smart, then use a lot of big words that no one understands and make it real complex. If your mission is to get your point across, use simple words. This is where ego comes in again. If you're trying to sound smart, you're off your mission. Don't try to sound smart. Try to convey great information.

Jargon is terrible. If you see jargon or acronyms, get rid of them. Don't assume that people get your acronyms.

My homework for you just to be observant about what has an impact on you. What subject lines got you to open an email? That's a little talking point, by the way. That subject line is a talking point. You can reinforce it in the email, but what gets them to open the email? That's your first talking point. If you open an email that you would normally not open because of a subject line, look at it. Think about what made you want to open it.

Look around at billboards. I love to drive down the interstate and look at billboards and especially the ones for which I have no idea what they're trying to say. There are too many words. There's a picture of something. I have no idea what it's conveying. It cracks me up. Bad billboards are wasted money. They're wasting all their energy, and they didn't convey anything. Typically, it's because they're trying to convey too much. You'll see them while driving and say, "I don't know what they're selling." Look at the ones at which you say, "I know exactly what they're selling," and notice the big differences. I really want you to start looking around the world. It'll be fun.

The last point I have for you is what songs stick in your head? What's that rhythm, those rhythmic words? Earworms are created typically because of the rhyme, rhythm and fluidity. That's really a next generation talking point. It's really hard to create that kind of fluid poetic feel to talking points. If you can get there, you are like next gen, PhD level advanced. Once again, I'm not telling you to write "smart." I'm telling you to write clearly, concisely and fluidly, which I think is smart.

SECTION VII:
MEDIA TRAINING

In my previous book I lay out many of the rules you should follow in dealing with the media. While these rules are fundamental when dealing with a crisis, they are also very helpful when dealing with the media in general. I have also found that in many of my speeches dealing with recruiting students, the conversation turns to the envitiable discussion of dealing with the reporters and developing other speeches. This meant I had a choice, I either try to push people to my other book, or I take the key points of my media training course and simply add them here. I have chosen the latter as I believe this provides the most all-inclusive tome on building a great reputation, which of course leads to more students. What follows is a summary of those rules I believe you will find most valuable.

NEVER BEHIND THE DESK

Don't do interviews sitting behind a desk. Just don't

I could spend page after page explaining why a desk separates you from the audience and why it makes you look unapproachable, but, frankly, I'm sick of writing these rules, so just don't!

RULE 2

DEVELOP RAPID RESPONSE TEAM

No one can see around every corner. No one can see or identify every landmine in front of them. There's no such thing as a strategist who can strategize on every element and every front. More often than not, it takes a team of people to identify potential problems, develop work arounds, in order for you to meet with success.

Now, I know that some people believe they can be an army of one, and maybe some of you actually can see around many corners and really establish all the problems and all the potential crises and all the disruptions that occur way ahead of time. But there's still the issue of the fishbowl, so to speak. What I mean by the fishbowl is that emotional fight-or-flight mentality that kicks in that you're too close to the issue with little outside, realistic perspective, and you are thinking about this issue every single day. And those seven responses that we talked about earlier in the book are kicking in, those emotional responses of "Do I want to go beat it up, or do I want to run from it, or do I want to ignore it?" kick in.

To have a team of advisors around you to get you to continue to see the global bigger picture is paramount to your success. Not just in dealing with the media. This section is talking about rules on dealing with the media, but it's really rules on communicating your message in times of disruption, in a crisis. Having outside advisors and having internal advisors whom you can trust to really develop and think about all the particular issues is vital to you getting through the situation as cleanly as possible.

What do we mean by rapid response team? These are people who you can bring together in very short order. I mean the word rapid is key to this. Is it your right-hand person in your office? Is it your two partners? Is it your chief of staff? Is it one of your deputy superintendents? Is it two principals? Is it a couple board members? Is it a lawyer? Is it an accountant? All those people can be a part of this team. It's really a group of five to nine people. No more than nine, really. There's a real sweet spot in terms of getting enough creative opinions that they don't completely envelop you with too much information. It's nice enough that everyone's opinion is going to be heard because it's still a small enough group to cultivate and flesh out the issues every person presents.

When you get people who can provide you all this great information about a particular disruption, you come together. You discuss it. You flesh out their arguments, and then together you work on the solution or the overall strategy to wrap it up. These people should be on speed dial. You might even want to have them on a group text thread. Maybe you don't use it for months and years, and I really hope that's the case, but when you need them, you need them.

The key to a rapid response team is just a group of trusted advisors. They don't have to be in your employ. They don't have to work for your team. Maybe it's just a good friend, and you trust their judgment, and they're available, and you can break down the issue at hand quickly, and together you can figure out the strategies and tactics to move forward.

RULE 3

USE SILENCE

You have taken the time to develop powerful 3-2-1 messages points. You have learned to stay on message. You have even taken the time to educate your entire team on the mission to avoid mission drift. Don't screw it up by running your mouth when you're not supposed to.

When you're asked a tough question by the media, it's OK to take some time to gather your thoughts. I'm not talking about days or even minutes, but a few seconds is OK.

Practice being silent for a few seconds after someone asks you a question. Sometimes the awkward silence can be deafening to you, but it's better to pause to gather your thoughts than to derail your entire mission.

TIP: Always think before you speak.

RULE 4

LEARN WHEN TO SHUT UP

Learning to keep your mouth shut is more akin to staying on message than it is to silence. Typically, people hate to repeat the same talking points over and over, so they elect to expand their talking points and begin to ramble. This is not a good idea.

A great example of talking too much and pushing too far was during the 2000 New York Senatorial debate between Rick Lazio and Hillary Clinton.[3]

Lazio was well-prepared for the debate and was ready with a great talking point (at least in his opinion it must have been great). He was ready to attack his opponent on campaign finance reform. When the question was asked about "soft money," he pulled a pledge document out of his pocket and said he was prepared to sign a pledge that he would not accept soft money if Clinton would also sign it.

Lazio knew Clinton would never sign the pledge, and he hoped to trap her. I'm sure during his planning sessions, they hoped the story the next day would be that "Clinton refuses to sign pledge against soft money." But instead, Lazio could not keep his mouth shut. He kept pushing her to sign the document and even went so far as to cross the stage and get in her face. He came off hostile and acted like a bully. So the next day, the story was not about her failure to sign the pledge, it was about his rude behavior. His inability to stop talking cost him the debate and ultimately victory.

---

3 Caleb Rojas Castillo. "First Debate Clinton-Lazio, 2000 – Part 6." Online video clip. YouTube. YouTube, 22 February 2010. Web.

TIP: You have taken the time to prepare strong talking points. Ensure they are heard by staying on message and not expanding on them just to fill air-time.

RULE 5

CALL REPORTERS BACK

Please call reports back. I beg you. I'm amazed by the number of very successful people who believe if they hide from the media, it will help their situation. It's as if they expect the reporter not to write the story if they don't call back. If a reporter is calling, it's because a story is being written. You either sell your side of events, or you allow the reporter to write the story without your input. If you want any chance at getting your part of a story out, call reporters back.

TIP: The sooner you return the call, the better. Otherwise, the reporter may look for alternative sources of information, which may not be beneficial to you. Moreover, the longer you wait to return the call, the more likely the story is already finished by the time you call back. So return those calls as soon as possible. If you want your side of the story covered in the news, *you* have to share it with the press.

RULE 6

AVOID PERSONAL OPINIONS

I love living in the United States and having the freedom to speak my mind. But make no mistake, the freedom to speak your mind does not mean that you are free from the repercussion of voicing your opinions. Others are just as free to boycott your products or shop elsewhere. So before you say something extremely controversial, ensure you are prepared for the blowback, not just on *you* but also on your livelihood. I'm not suggesting you do not speak your mind; I just want you to prepare yourself for what could come from that.

Now, I want to make one very clear distinction: It is *imperative* that when you are speaking on behalf of a business or client that you avoid giving your personal opinion. You may think you are speaking for yourself, but if you are the spokesperson for a company, its CEO or even just speaking to the press with a company shirt on, people are going to connect your statement to the business, even if you claim it's just your personal opinion.

Once you start going down the road of providing your personal opinion, it's a slippery slope that will cause you to violate many other rules. You immediately get off your key message points; you're no longer staying focused on your main mission; and you're not using talking points to drive your message home. More than just violating other rules, your comments may have unintended consequences. Remember, you're speaking on behalf of lots of people now, not just yourself. They should have a say in what is presented, hence the development of the talking points. If you go off script, you may claim that it was just your opinion, but you no longer have that luxury–you are responsible for the entire team's success. So the best idea is to avoid giving personal opinions all together.

Also, please understand that this extends to your social media profiles. I still cannot figure out why so many people think that the use of social media will not affect their business lives. It's almost as if people believe the Internet is a safe place to say whatever stupid thought they have with no consequences. Every Facebook post, every Tweet, and every other social media post can and *will* be read by someone. If you're acting on behalf of your company in any capacity, keep your profiles free from your personal opinions about the crisis at hand.

TIP: Always remember that if you're speaking on someone else's behalf, keep your opinions to yourself. Instead of providing personal opinions, try pivoting like this: "Well, I'm speaking for the organization, not myself, and what we believe is . . ." If you are asked to speak about your personal opinion on an issue within the organization, don't fall for it. Keep your mouth shut.

RULE 7

ONLY MORONS SAY NO COMMENT

Yes, it's OK to ignore a question; it's OK to pivot to another answer; and it's even OK to say you do not know the answer, but the words "no comment" have a certain stigma attached to them that you just can't get rid of.

Let me put it another way. Assume you see your spouse having dinner with a mysterious stranger in a dimly lit restaurant. When you see your spouse back at home and ask them where they were, what would you think if they said "no comment?" What about a person being prosecuted for a crime that says "no comment?" Sure, we're not supposed to assume this means they're guilty, but most of our brains go in that direction, regardless of intent.

"No comment" leaves the listener with a gut reaction that you are hiding something. Our legal system allows people to exercise our right to plead the Fifth,[4] but the court of public opinion is not obligated to follow the same guidelines.

To be clear, I am not suggesting that you answer every question. I'm just recommending you don't use the actual words "no comment" in a crisis situation.

Like most rules, this one has an exception. If you actually *do* want to imply that you're withholding information, saying "no comment" is a great way to do that. A former politician and old friend of mine would often use this phrase on purpose to convey to the listener that he knew certain information or how a vote would play out on an important issue, but he would refuse

---

4 The Fifth Amendment to the U.S. Constitution's Bill of Rights contains several protections against government intrusion, including the clause regarding self-incrimination. This was developed to prevent anyone from being forced to testify against him or herself, leading to the maxim that someone is "innocent until proven guilty."

to reveal the details, often smiling at the camera while saying, "no comment." As this situation wasn't crisis-related, he was in the clear to use "no comment" in that manner.

TIP: Here are some good pivot phrases to use instead of "no comment."

That's not what I'm here to discuss

I'm unable to talk about that because

No (if it's the truth)

I wouldn't use that choice of words. If you are asking whether . . . . I can tell you that

I don't have all the facts to be able to answer that question accurately. But I can tell you that . . .

RULE 8
"I DON'T KNOW"

Reporters will ask all types of questions. Big, broad questions, super detailed questions and questions that are way off topic. No one expects you to have the answers to every question at your fingertips, but sometimes our egos come in to play and stop us from admitting that we do not know everything.

Sometimes the best answer really is "I do not know." It's honest and it stops you from guessing, which can cause all sorts of problems down the road. The best approach is to be honest and let them know you will get the information as quickly as possible and report back. It's OK to not have all the answers right then and there.

However, an even better approach (if you can manage it) is to pivot to an answer that you *do* know that's related to the question. For instance, if you are asked, "What is the number of X?" and you don't know, you can say, "What I can tell you about the number is that it's been growing dramatically because..." and get right back to something you *do* know so that your credibility is not questioned.[5]

Please remember that this rule *does not* relieve you of your responsibility to prepare. People will expect you to know the answers to the most important and relevant questions. You must have those facts and figures ready to go when the media comes around.

---

5 Spiegel, Alix. "How Politicians Get Away With Dodging The Question." *National Public Radio*. National Public Radio, 3 October 2012. Web.

RULE 9
BEYOND YES-OR-NO QUESTIONS

Have you ever been asked a yes-or-no question? Did you feel trapped? That was probably on purpose. Reporters will often use yes-or-no scenarios to trap you into an unflattering soundbite. Lawyers use yes-or-no questions during cross examination to box witnesses into a corner. It stops a person from explaining their side of events.

The media and the public at large may use the same tool to stop you from explaining your side of the story. Do not fall for the trap. You have the right to answer questions in a way that benefits you.

For example, a police director could be asked, "Hasn't there been an increase in violence over the last few years?" or "Haven't there been several examples of questionable police conduct over the last few months?"

Instead of answering with a yes or no, the director should answer, "Every big metropolitan city has issues with violence. As law enforcement professionals, we are doing everything we can to protect our city and serve our city's people. You may have heard some things recently about police officer misconduct. We take it seriously and investigate every situation that we are faced with, and each party responsible will be disciplined appropriately."

The yes-or-no question can get some people off message, but don't let it get you. Stick to your 3-2-1 message points. You can alter the wording of the responses, but not the themes. Also, watch your tone and stay calm even if you're irritated.

TIP: You are in charge of your communications. Do not let the type of question you're asked stop you from getting your message out. You are not in a court of law. You can answer as you like. Take every opportunity to sell your side of the story. Responding with only yes or no may fail to fully explain your situation. Don't feel boxed in. Sell, sell, sell!

RULE 10
LEARN TO INTERRUPT

Being polite is one thing, but getting walked over is another. You must find the balance between letting people ask questions, responding in a calm manner, and allowing a person to roll right over you.

This is exceptionally difficult when you're being interviewed live on television or in front of a public meeting. The best way to determine if it's time to interrupt and shut down the line of questioning is to know how you typically respond in these situations.

If you're the kind of person who lets things slide and typically avoids conflict, I suggest you jump in before you are ready. If you are a hot head, impatient, and rarely let other people finish a thought before you react, cool your jets and exercise more patience before you interrupt. Most of us probably fall in the middle of the spectrum, so listen to your gut, pause, and then decide if you should act.

TIP: If a mom does it, then it must be right, right? Some may think this is surprising, but the website Modern Mom has the best tips I've seen on how to interrupt politely:

Step One: Implement body language to signal to the speaker that you have something to add to the conversation. Look the speaker directly in the eye, and he may recognize that you want to speak. If making eye contact isn't enough to get the speaker's attention, raise your hand slightly, sit forward on your seat, cough quietly or clear your throat.

Step Two: Wait patiently and avoid interrupting abruptly. If possible, wait until the speaker completes a thought or pauses

---

between sentences. If there is a lull in the conversation, use the opportunity to interject your comment, question or opinion.

Step Three: Speak clearly, using polite, non threatening phrases. Be assertive but polite. For example, enter the conversation by saying, "Pardon me," "Just a moment," "Excuse me," "I'm sorry to interrupt," or "Actually . . ." Alternatively, ask the speaker if you can interrupt by saying, "May I ask a question?" or "Can I jump in here for a moment?"

Step Four: Give the speaker your full attention and wait for him to stop and acknowledge your request to speak. Stay on topic and make your point clearly and succinctly. Thank the speaker, and then allow him to continue.

Step Five: Avoid unnecessary interruptions. Don't finish the speaker's sentences and don't interrupt to unnecessarily correct the speaker. Don't monopolize the conversation. If necessary, set a time to discuss the matter in more detail.

Step Six: Consider the other person's feelings. Save sensitive comments for a private conversation. If your comments aren't important enough to justify the interruption, keep the comments to yourself.

Endnotes for this Tip Box can be found here: [6]

6 Dyer, M.H. "How to Interrupt Politely." *Modern Mom*. Modern Mom, n.d. Web.

RULE 11
BODY LANGUAGE MATTERS

Body language is just as important (and sometimes even more important) than the words you actually say. Many experts claim that nonverbal communications can impact an audience more than our words. Volumes of books have been written on this topic, and I would encourage you to read them or even take a course if you want to improve your public speaking ability.

I do, however, want to cover a few landmines that could get you in trouble—especially if you are defensive or upset, and the media is in your face. I understand that I am starting to nitpick a little with this rule, but my job is to protect you and your reputation. The one action that always comes off looking bad is when a person tries to block the camera with their hand. Reporters love those types of shots and love people running from the camera even more.

Running or putting your hands up to block the camera comes off incredibly defensive and makes for a good story in its own right. If you are not prepared to answer questions, just say so and schedule another time to answer questions, then walk off slowly and continue to repeat that you will do your research and be back to answer the questions. But please, do not run and do not block the camera.

TIP: Here are a few tips to improve your nonverbal communication:

Use your gestures to create more impact. Gestures can emphasize key points. The best way to ensure you use gestures is to keep your hands free. Do not place them in your pockets or hold a cup of coffee. Freeing your hands up will allow you to use them to help express your thoughts. Of course, like every rule, you can take this too far. Don't stand up there and look like a windmill.

Watch Unhappy Resting Face.[7] A few people are afflicted with this, and if you are, you usually know. It's when your resting face, the face you have on when you're zoning out or not paying particular attention to anything, looks upset or angry. You could be in a perfectly good mood, but your face says otherwise. If you have this problem, you need to work on it in a mirror or with a coach. Of course, the other side of the spectrum can also get you in trouble. If you smile all the time (especially when nervous), and you're talking about a serious subject, you can come across as uncaring. Facial expressions matter.

Stand up. To ensure you are able to use gestures and show energy, never do a press conference or make an announcement sitting down. Social psychologist Amy Cuddy's research into power poses covers in great detail ways to use poses to ensure you take better control.[8]

---

7 Terminology rephrased from original presentation.

8 Cuddy, Amy. "Your body language shapes who you are." *TED*. TED. June 2012. Web.

RULE 12

THE CAMERA IS
ALWAYS ON

It's amazing how many seasoned professionals forget this rule. Simply put, everything you say can and will be used against you. Even if you think you're just being cute or funny, your words will be your own downfall more often than the actions of others will be.

Think of it like this: Do not say or write anything that you do not want to see on the cover of the local newspaper or headlining the nightly news. This is especially true in dealing with the media. I don't care if you think you have a great relationship with the reporter, it's their job to report on anything that will help sell their stories and get people to watch their programs. And let's face it, people love to watch accidents, and they love to watch people mess up. From forgetting to turn a microphone off, to assuming they were not being recorded, to emailing something to the wrong person, many people have been destroyed by their own words. If you do not say it or write it, they cannot print it.

Let me tell you about two of my favorite examples of major mess-ups in this category. First, in 2010, then California Republican Senate nominee Carly Fiorina was caught on camera before an interview talking trash about Senator Barbara Boxer. I guess she thought the cameras weren't on, despite the fact that she was sitting in a TV studio with a microphone attached. She was speaking to the interviewer as if they were having a private conversation and made a snide comment about her political opponent's hairstyle. Needless to say the video got out, went viral and destroyed her campaign. [9]

---

9 CNN. "CNN: Pre on-air bloopers." Online video clip. *YouTube*. YouTube, 10 June 2010. Web.

My other favorite example was in 2006 when Kyra Phillips, an anchor for CNN was wired with a microphone but either forgot she was wired or didn't turn it off, and made some pretty disparaging comments about men in general and her sister-in-law in particular. The kicker? Her mic was broadcasting on top of then President G. W. Bush's speech one year after hurricane Katrina.[10]

Folks, please don't forget that the camera is on and the mics are picking up audio at every moment.

---

10 snosons. "CNN's Kyre Phillips Forgets to Turn off Mic." Online video clip. *YouTube*. YouTube, 29 August 2006. Web.

RULE 13
CONSISTENT MESSAGES

The toughest thing about communicating is, well, communicating. It takes time and effort to update your employees, stakeholders and the public at large with relevant information, just like it takes time and effort to talk to your spouse after a long and difficult day at work.

However, the more consistent you are, the more likely people will hear and understand your message, making the endless communication worth it. This rule ties in with keeping your message simple and pivoting back to your main 3-2-1 message points. The key is repeating the same overall message throughout all of your communications on an issue. Don't, however, repeat the same message point word-for-word over and over. Listen to the questions you're asked and let them guide your responses as you stay consistent. Use different wording but keep the same main points.

Consistency is all about keeping control of the situation and staying on point with your messages. I understand that you have a bunch of points that the public needs to know, but please realize that your audience has a life outside of your crisis. They are busy with their own jobs and families. They are simply too busy to listen to everything you have to say. If you want them to hear something, you better make it simple and say it over and over in the hopes that they will finally pick it up. You *must* fight off the urge to come up with some new message. Staying consistent gives you a better chance to reach your audience.

TIP: Your internal and external messages should be the same. What you tell employees should be the same as what you tell the media. If not, somebody will get bad information, and your crisis will only be compounded. Assign one person on your team to review and approve outgoing message points to ensure consistency.

RULE 14

STAY AHEAD OF THE MEDIA

You are in control of your story as long as you are the one releasing the facts. Often, people in crisis hope the facts will not come out. They hope that if they stay quiet and hide, that the truth and the media will just go away. But once you are in the middle of a mess and the spotlight is on you, it's more likely that *all* the facts will come out, whether you like it or not. The only thing you can control is how they come out and how they are presented. You simply cannot hide from the mess, but you can control the rhythm and how the information is released. By releasing information, even negative information, you start to gain control and can set the right tone.

Let's dissect a typical crisis situation: A company called Kid Cribs, Inc. sells baby cribs. Kid Cribs buys their baby beds from a manufacturer that isn't inspected regularly. News comes out that Kid Cribs' beds are made with lead paint. Kid Cribs' CEO investigates the situation and learns that five additional products they sell also contain lead. What should Kid Cribs do?

In many situations, the company will not want to release the news about the additional five products. Instead, Kid Cribs (and most other companies) would prefer to fix the issue and hope that the press never catches on to the buried information. However, what inevitably happens is that the media *does* learn because it's their job to dig up information. So the media reports in another story each time they find one of Kid Cribs' lead-infused products. This drags the story on for months, causing severe damage to their businesses reputation.

A better solution would have been to get the information out upfront, get one or two bad stories written, and resolve all outstanding issues at once. Thereby allowing you to move forward as quickly as possible. Disclosures of that nature also show that the company is transparent and cares about its customers. The public can forgive a mistake you're working to fix, but they will be less forgiving if they think you're hiding something.

VIII:
NOTES